"Marriage on the rocks? Wond
your marriage? Linda Rooks has written HOPE and HELP into your future!
This book is a healing balm for one of life's very unwelcome, unwanted, and
unbelievably difficult journeys. It's a must-read for anyone finding themselves struggling to hold on to his or her marriage."

Pam Farrel, Author of forty-five books including bestselling *Men Are
Like Waffles, Women Are Like Spaghetti*; codirector of Love-Wise

"Practical, powerful, confidence-building, and enlightening describe this book
by Linda Rooks. Her wisdom is greatly needed and will embolden those who
feel lost and hopeless in the midst of marital separation and abandonment. As
lay counselors, we will be recommending *Fighting for Your Marriage While
Separated* knowing it will give others biblical hope in God's care and the Holy
Spirit's empowering."

Kathy Collard Miller and Larry Miller, Lay counselors,
speakers, and authors of many books including *Never Ever Be
the Same*

"Powerful! Practical! Biblical! *Fighting for Your Marriage While Separated* walks
couples step-by-step through separation to possible reconciliation. Linda Rooks,
with a heart filled with understanding and hope, shares biblical truth, her own
three-year separation, and real-time stories of brokenhearted couples. A must-
read for anyone contemplating the end of their marriage. You may not fix your
marriage, but God can!"

Elaine W. Miller, International speaker; author of *We All Married
Idiots: Three Things You Will Never Change About Your Marriage and
Ten Things You Can*

"When you open this book, you enter into an intimate conversation with a
trusted friend. Linda Rooks warmly extends a hand of compassionate support to the brokenhearted spouse, offering both biblical hope and wisdom.
With great purpose, she draws upon countless years of serving hurting
spouses. We highly recommend *Fighting for Your Marriage While Separated*
not only to spouses in crisis, but to counselors, pastors, and other marriage
champions."

Clint and Penny A. Bragg, Authors of *Marriage Off Course: Trusting
God in the Desert of Unwanted Separation or Divorce*

"Linda Rooks not only understands what it means to fight for a marriage—she understands what it takes to win the war that separated couples face. The book you are about to read is filled with hope, direction, and 'Heart Work' exercises that will help guide you through whatever battle you are facing in your marriage. A tremendous book we will have on our resource list for every separated person."

> **Joe and Michelle Williams**, Authors of *Yes, Your Marriage Can Be Saved*; founders of Marriage 911 God's Way Ministry

"As a counselor, I've witnessed firsthand the heartbreak of a person who wants to save his or her marriage with someone who has no interest in reconciling. Linda Rooks has not only successfully navigated this confusing, complicated path herself but offers hope through her true-life stories and excellent strategies. While making no guarantees, *Fighting for Your Marriage* lays out helpful do's and don'ts, showing that a restored marriage is possible."

> **Georgia Shaffer**, PA Licensed Psychologist; professional certified coach; author; founder of ReBUILD, small-group internet coaching for the separated and divorced

"Anyone who is dealing with separation in marriage or works with those who are in deep marital distress can benefit from reading *Fighting for Your Marriage While Separated*. Linda Rooks shares her story of separation and reconciliation with vulnerability, encouragement, and hope. She doesn't offer a quick fix, but gives practical wisdom for navigating the difficulties, as if talking with you over a cup of coffee."

> **Nancy Kay Grace**, Speaker; author of *The Grace Impact*; member of the board of directors for United Marriage Encounter; former presenter for United Marriage Encounter

"Fighting for your marriage is absolutely essential, even while separated! God has a process and a plan for our lives, and waiting and going through a wilderness period may be just that plan for a time! Linda's book is an incredible resource for walking this out, keeping you focused, and potentially waiting for God's direction for your marriage!"

> **Jeff & Cheryl Scruggs**, Speakers; biblical counselors; authors of *I Do Again*; founders of Hope Matters Marriage Ministries and *Thriving Beyond Belief* podcast for women

FIGHTING FOR YOUR MARRIAGE WHILE SEPARATED

A PRACTICAL GUIDE FOR THE BROKENHEARTED

Linda W. Rooks

New
Growth
Press
WWW.NEWGROWTHPRESS.COM

New Growth Press, Greensboro, NC 27404
www.newgrowthpress.com

Scripture quotations marked NIV are from *The Holy Bible, New International Version®. NIV®.* Copyright ©1973, 1978, 1984, 2011 by Biblica, Inc.® Used by permission. All rights reserved worldwide.

Scripture quotations marked NASB are taken from the New American Standard Bible®. Copyright © 1960, 1962, 1963, 1968, 1971, 1972, 1973, 1975, 1977, 1995 by The Lockman Foundation.

Scripture quotations marked NKJV are taken from the New King James Version®. Copyright © 1982 by Thomas Nelson. Used by permission. All rights reserved.

Scripture quotations marked TLB are taken from The Living Bible copyright © 1971 by Tyndale House Foundation. Used by permission of Tyndale House Publishers Inc., Carol Stream, Illinois 60188. All rights reserved.

Scripture quotations marked NRSV are taken from the New Revised Standard Version Bible, copyright © 1989 the Division of Christian Education of the National Council of the Churches of Christ in the United States of America. Used by permission. All rights reserved.

Scripture quotations marked MSG are taken from The Message. Copyright © 1993, 1994, 1995, 1996, 2000, 2001, 2002 by Eugene H. Peterson.

Cover Design: Faceout Books, faceoutstudio.com
Interior Typesetting and eBook: Lisa Parnell, lparnell.com

ISBN: 978-1-948130-53-0 (Print)
ISBN: 978-1-948130-54-7 (eBook)

Library of Congress Cataloging-in-Publication Data
Names: Rooks, Linda W., author.
Title: Fighting for your marriage while separated : a practical guide for the
    brokenhearted / Linda W. Rooks.
Description: Greensboro : New Growth Press, 2019. | Includes bibliographical
    references.
Identifiers: LCCN 2018056000 (print) | LCCN 2018061507 (ebook) |
    ISBN 9781948130547 (ebook) | ISBN 9781948130530 (trade paper)
Subjects: LCSH: Separated people—Religious life. | Marriage—Religious aspects—
    Christianity. | Reconciliation—Religious aspects—Christianity.
Classification: LCC BV4596.S39 (ebook) | LCC BV4596.S39 R665 2019 (print) |
    DDC 248.8/46—dc23
LC record available at https://lccn.loc.gov/2018056000

Printed in Canada

26 25 24 23 22 21 20 19   1 2 3 4 5

Contents

Dedication

I still remember my husband looking up at me from the papers I had handed him, a mixture of wonder and grace settling over his demeanor. "This is a Romans 8:28," he said. "This is the way God will bring good from our pain—by using our story to help others."

The papers he had just read chronicled my healing from the pain of our separation, and since my husband's first reading of those words, his enthusiasm for passing healing words onto those in hurting marriages has not wavered. His support and encouragement has kept me going through many months of writing and many years of ministry.

And so, to you, my husband, Marv—the man I have loved over these many years—I dedicate this book. Thank you for your love, support, and encouragement, which has enabled us to share with others the hope we found together and the story of the renewed love we enjoy today.

"And we know that in all things
God works for the good of those who love him,
who have been called according to his purpose."
ROMANS 8:28

Acknowledgments

In acknowledging those who played a part in bringing this book about, I must begin with you, my readers and those who have sat in our marriage classes week after week. Time and time again, your stories and your lives have taught me about God's grace, his redemption, and his power to transform. Your tears and the pain you shared with me along with God's wondrous promise in Romans 8:28 serve as the seeds of inspiration for what follows on these pages. For, indeed, "all things God works for the good of those who love him, who have been called according to his purpose." Your perseverance and your willingness to let God make changes is a beautiful testimony. I particularly want to thank each and every one of you who allowed me to share your stories so others could find hope. Your honesty and vulnerability shine a light on what is possible with God to provide hope for those in hurting marriages.

Secondly, I must thank my husband, Marv, whose enthusiasm and support for this book kept me on track. Thanks for your faithfulness in reading each and every chapter, sharing your thoughts with me, and being my consultant when it was challenging to make decisions.

A special thanks also to my daughter Julie Wolf for sharing her story as a teen dealing with my husband's and my separation, and for contributing to the chapter on "Protecting Your Child's Heart" by sharing her experience as a mental health counselor.

And thanks to those who spent time with me in person or on the phone, sharing their professional expertise. Robert S. Paul shared his vast knowledge and experience about the uniqueness of marital counseling. John Tardonia helped me address the issue of physical abuse. P. J. and Frank Turner gave me a workable plan for those with addictive spouses. Pastor Carl Stephens offered his wise counsel. Cheryl Scruggs advised on reconciliation after divorce. My appreciation also goes to William Donahue for allowing me to share from his insightful writings on marriage counseling

Thanks also to Barbara Juliani for believing in this project and bringing it to fruition, to Ruth Castle who helped me sharpen my focus, and to Mollie Turbeville for her fine-tuning.

To Lyle Cain, thanks for rescuing me from computer stress on a number of occasions, and to my friends in Word Weavers, thanks for many helpful suggestions and critiques for portions of my manuscript.

Finally, thanks to my agent Jonathan Clements for enduring with me through good times and bad.

A Personal Note
to My Readers

While my own tears and my own breaking heart were ground zero for my first book, *Broken Heart on Hold*, it has been the tears and heartbreaking stories from readers and those in our crisis marriage classes that are ground zero for *Fighting for Your Marriage While Separated*.

As I have watched them grapple with mind-numbing circumstances and listened to their stories, I have learned from them. I have seen them overcome incredible obstacles, surmount impossible odds, gently woo reluctant and prodigal spouses, and stand strong when divorce threatened to bring them down. I have seen the beauty of hearts resurrected and lives renewed, regardless of the results, when God becomes the center. Many of these stories (with prior consent) can be found throughout these pages.

If you, my reader, are new to this battle and feel you are stepping into it alone, the true and heartfelt stories sprinkled throughout this book will reassure you there is hope for you and your marriage. Although these stories use fictional names to protect identities, the enthusiasm each of these people showed for giving to you what God has given to them has been a beautiful testimony of God's healing grace.

Wherever you are in the battle for your marriage, this is your book. These chapters are answers to your questions. The tears and pain many others have shared with me through the years have prepared the soil and watered the seeds for what will be shared in the following pages. You are not alone.

So, let's get started. Your Commander is calling, and it's time to charge into battle. Together, we are going to fight for your marriage.

Chapter 1

Reacting to Your New Situation

Though he has been gone six months now, I still wake during the night with that sense of fear, sick to my stomach, enveloped with a stinging heat in my body. It's the most horrible feeling I have ever encountered. I suspect you know very well this feeling, and all the other feelings and sensations I suffer. I have, for the first time in my life, begun to have anxiety attacks. Can I tell you how scared I am? I have, at this point, lost my husband of nearly twenty-seven years. If you have any suggestions to help me learn to take my focus off of my husband and my great grief and pain, I would love to hear from you. — *Sarah*

With a crumbling marriage at your feet, reckless and thoughtless words swirling through your head, and a gnawing pain eating at your heart, where do you go from here?

What does it look like to fight for your marriage? Is saving it even possible?

The shock that comes when your spouse walks out the door or announces a desire for divorce shakes you, the one left behind, to the core of your being. It's a moment of panic. Of desperation. Every fiber in your body cries out for action. You feel like that proverbial chicken whose head was cut off. You can't think, but every muscle in your body is ready for action.

But what action?

What do you do?

How do you fight for your marriage?

In the emails I get from readers, I hear the heartache. Each story is very different, but the pain bleeds from each sentence and paragraph. My heart grieves for those who write as they tell about suffering through an agony I know all too well because of my own three-year separation a number of years ago.

Because my own marriage was restored and because I have been able to work with so many others to reconcile their marriages, I can confidently tell you it is possible to fight for your marriage and win—even when your spouse has turned away from you.

But what does it look like to fight for your marriage?

FROM NEVER TO FOREVER

Alexandra could not eat or sleep. Bill would not talk to her or answer her calls. When she found him at the house he was renting, he refused to let her inside.

From the moment she found her husband standing beside his Hyundai Sonata packed with all his belongings, her world turned upside down.

"What are you doing?" she asked.

"I've been telling you for months I can't handle it anymore."

"Where are you moving? When are you coming back?"

"I rented a house," Bill said. "I don't know what's going to happen. I need space. I need time."

During that first month after he left, all Alexandra could do was cry. She lost twenty pounds. When they eventually went to counseling, Bill told her week after week he did not see them getting back together— ever. He agreed to keep things as normal as possible for the kids and reluctantly spent the holidays with her and occasionally went on outings as a family. Bill was adamant, however, that this was only for the children. They were not getting back together.

Grasping for something to relieve her pain, Alexandra decided to go to church even though her past experiences had not been particularly pleasant or meaningful. This new church seemed different though. From the first moment she stepped inside, she felt at home. She felt God's presence and a new peace. As a result, Alexandra started seeking God with all her heart. She found a prayer partner who continually lifted her up to God. She attended a class at the church called Marriage 911 where she saw God leading her to make changes in herself. She earnestly asked God to show her what she needed to do.

Even as Alexandra began to change, however, Bill regularly dashed her hopes by saying there would be no reconciliation.

Still, Alexandra pressed on with God and clung to hope. Whenever she engaged in conversations with her husband, she sought God's guidance. Alexandra stopped pushing and began to show Bill a new respect that reflected a fresh understanding of his needs as a man and as her husband. When they had arguments, she realized pressing her point until she could prove she was right was not productive. Instead, she stepped back and put everything in the hands of her Savior.

Eventually, Bill saw the changes in her and began initiating times for them to get together and talk while doing things they both enjoyed. But he still insisted he had no interest in ever reconciling.

One day he asked to come over and talk.

"I think it's time," he said.

"Time for what? What do you mean it's time?"

"I don't see us getting back together. I think it's time to file. I've saved some money in my savings and my 401(k). I'll cash it out. Half of it is yours. I'll do what I can to help you. But it's time to file for divorce. This isn't going to work out."

Although stunned, Alexandra remained calm. "If that's what you want, I cannot stop you, but I'm not going to file or take the first step. You'll have to do it. You're going to have to sit down and talk to the kids too. I don't want any part of it. God isn't telling me it's done yet."

Alexandra knew she had done everything she could to save her marriage. She had talked and tried to convince him. She'd cried. She'd read books and had gone to classes. She'd sought counsel from others and made serious changes. Now it was up to God. It had been two years, and there was nothing more to do.

"God, if this is what you want," she prayed, "then give me the strength." With those words, she finally let go and surrendered it all to the Lord. If Bill wanted to end the marriage, she could not stop him. Despite her pain, she was at peace.

Because they had lost their house, Alexandra found a small apartment for her and the kids. She cobbled together a few new pieces of furniture and decorated the walls with Scripture art.

During the next few months, a series of accidents and surgeries in the family shone a light on Alexandra's new demeanor. She was calmer and more at peace. Her new independence and ability to handle all the tumult caught Bill's attention. Over the next few months, Bill's heart began to change, and so did his decision about the divorce.

He began dropping by the house on a regular basis. He invited her to dinner and on bike rides. As he saw Alexandra truly let go and prepare to move on, his heart began to open to her. On the morning of Ash Wednesday as he lay in bed praying, he felt the Spirit saying, "Trust me for forty days and allow my Spirit to go before you. Go back to your family."

Bill fell in love with her all over again and moved back in. Thankfully, he had never filed for divorce.

The way each person handles a separation can make the difference in the outcome. You may mess up and not do it right at first, but if you can eventually give it to God, you might be surprised at how God works it all together for good as in the story of Alexandra and Bill above. Even as you fight this battle for your marriage, however, it's important to realize God's idea of victory in your life may not be the same as yours. A restored marriage may be part of that victory, but it's not guaranteed. However, as you assemble your armor and learn new strategies, God will give you the strength you need to become all he wants you to be so you can enjoy the victory ahead, whatever form it takes.

The following principles provide an important and proven strategy for those who eventually find reconciliation and healing. Take these steps prayerfully. Never step out on your "to-do" list or walk into battle without listening for guidance from the Commander. God will guide you step-by-step.

Give Space

If your husband or wife left, your first intentional response should be to give your partner space. Spouses who leave are usually confused and need space to sort themselves out. They may be running from conflict, which may be conflict in the home or a conflict raging within themselves. Either way, chasing after them with questions or accusations only pushes them further away.

Although your heart may be crying out for answers, a spouse who has left probably has no answers for you. Chances are your mate doesn't even know himself what he wants, and any attempt to respond to your questions will likely produce something you don't want to hear. However, if you can give him time to clear his head, your partner may come to a better place where answers will be more gratifying.

But how do you give space? For most of you this is an extremely difficult assignment and goes against the desperate cries of your heart. How do you fight for your marriage if you have no contact with your spouse? In this battle, you have a Commander whose strategy far exceeds your own. Take this time to look to him. Let him guard your heart and begin your healing while you take necessary measures to move into a better place emotionally.

Giving space to the one who has left means that for a period of time you don't call, email, or text unless you need to discuss something significant. When you do have contact, don't put pressure on your partner or talk about issues. Instead, pray for your spouse and use this time to get closer to God. Let your husband or wife contact you. Wait and pray.

After a period of time with no interaction and after praying for guidance, you might extend an olive branch to just say hello and see how your mate is doing. But don't call to put pressure on. Simply make it a friendly exchange and say something positive. Your purpose is not to create a standoff but to provide time for her to clear her head. After giving your partner space for a while, it's appropriate to send a message that says I'm thinking of you. Give her something positive to hang onto.

That "In Love" Feeling

Why, you ask, should I have any hope at this point if my spouse said he doesn't love me anymore? After all, I can't change his feelings.

Having now been in marriage ministry for so many years, I have found this to be one of the most common statements I hear from women whose husbands have left. With hearts breaking, they repeat to me their husband's words: he doesn't love her anymore or he isn't "in love" with her anymore. Sometimes, he adds that he doesn't think he ever loved her. A few words bring her whole world crashing down upon her. In the case of a man whose wife has left, it seems more typical for her to say something like, "I don't know if I love you anymore."

The amazing, but undeniable truth, however, is these feelings can change. What your spouse feels right now may be very different in six months. Feelings are only temporary, and people make a tremendous mistake when they allow emotions to shape their decisions.

In our marriage classes, my husband, Marv, drives this point home on a regular basis to those in attendance.

"Feelings change," he says. He even writes the words on the whiteboard at the front of the class and underlines them to emphasize his claim. He knows the truth of this firsthand because many years ago, when we were separated, he was one of those spouses who left and questioned his feelings of love for me. After three years of separation, we reconciled. Today he has no doubt and tells me daily he loves me. We have seen this turnaround to be true with many other couples as well.

Feelings change. That "in love," euphoric feeling, in fact, is scientifically considered a very temporary state, which lasts anywhere from three to thirty-six months.[1] Dr. Michael R. Liebowitz, author of *The Chemistry of Love*, calls it the "attraction" stage of love and describes the feeling of love as a powerful disturbance of our normal brain chemistry. "Love is a brain bath of dopamine and norepinephrine," he writes. But this feeling of love does not last long.

In the *New York Times* article, "Chemical Connections: Pathways of Love," Glenn Collins continues the quote from Liebowitz. "In the natural process of acclimation, lovers achieve a measure of toleration or adaptation to each other, and the thrill is gone. Yet in our culture we demand that our relationships continue to be romantic. I think it's because the media constantly portray only one sort of love as desirable—attraction, rather than attachment."[2]

As a consequence of these beliefs, people who expect "in love" feelings to continue will have to go from one relationship to another every few years. That, of course, is not the purpose of a relationship. People need to build something deeper, and this comes in the second stage of love. Liebowitz calls this "attachment," which is "associated with warm feelings that may be calming or comforting."[3]

Eventually, as your spouse has time to process his feelings, his mixed-up emotions may begin to calm down, and feelings of love toward you may return. Until he or she finds personal healing, however, your mate probably won't be able to respond to you with the love you want. How you handle this stage of the battle can make a big difference in what happens next. Waiting with restraint is extremely hard but important, and at this point it begins by giving time.

Give It Time

As you struggle through this confusion from one day to the next, you want to ask your spouse over and over, "What are you going to do? When are you coming home?" You could even be tempted to make ultimatums so she understands you will not wait forever. You want her to decide to come home. You want this pain to end. And if it's not going to end, then at least you want closure. What you don't want is for the pain to continue. What you don't want is a broken heart on hold.

But God's ways are not our ways. "'For my thoughts are not your thoughts, neither are your ways my ways,' declares the LORD. 'As the heavens are higher than the earth, so are my ways higher than your ways and my thoughts than your thoughts'" (Isaiah 55:8–9).

While feelings can definitely change, it takes time for this to happen. You can't rush it. Give God the time he needs to help you and your spouse make the necessary changes to bring about a truly restored marriage.

God uses everything for his purposes. His ways are perfect. If you want to see true healing in the lives of you and your partner, you must surrender this time to God. Do not put restrictions on him. God is an omniscient, powerful, and everlasting God, the Alpha and Omega, the first and the last. Time to him is like the blink of an eye. Give it to him.

Focus on God

Because of the intensity of what is happening, it's easy to become obsessed with your circumstances. But obsession will only make the situation worse. At a marriage conference I attended, marriage therapist Michele Weiner-Davis shared a five-word slogan that can be pivotal in your thinking. I share it continually in the marriage classes Marv and I lead: "What you focus on expands."[4]

Whatever you allow yourself to think about becomes more prominent in your mind and your emotions. If you fixate on the confusion of your negative circumstances, it will consume you, but if you focus on God, he will fill your heart with his peace.

To keep your sanity, put your spouse on the back burner and keep your focus completely on God, your Commander in chief. Do not allow your husband or wife to define who you are.

Use this time to get alone with God. Let him strengthen you to give you the necessary armor for the battle. Life is a journey of change and growth. During this period of your life, as you come closer to the Lord and put your trust completely in God, he can show you any changes he wants you to make that will fulfill you as a person and perhaps bring peace and healing to your marriage. Proverbs 3:5–6 says, "Trust in the LORD with all your heart, and lean not on your own understanding; In all your ways acknowledge Him, and He shall direct your paths" (NKJV). God has a plan for you, and he will guide you through this battle. Humbly seek God's direction.

To focus on God and your relationship with him, spend quality and quantity time in his Word and in seeking him through prayer. Tune in to radio and television teachers or tap into online teaching resources. Read Christian books. Keep Christian praise music playing throughout the day and sing along with it. Read or reread *Broken Heart on Hold* as a devotional book to keep yourself strong spiritually. Try to identify in yourself habits, reactions, or behaviors that may be a hindrance to a good marital relationship. Do not do this to win your spouse back. Do it to live out who God says you are and who he's called you to be.

Nurture Yourself

Chances are the stress in your marriage has prevented you from doing a lot of things you used to enjoy. Rekindle some of those interests you may have put aside. Give yourself permission to develop new talents and interests you enjoy.

While God offers you his love and peace to bind up the wounds of your heart, you are responsible for making positive choices that are healthy and satisfying to take care of yourself. Scripture says to "guard your heart, for everything you do flows from it" (Proverbs 4:23). God wants to lead you into a fruitful and productive life, even in the midst of the chaos surrounding you. As he provides protection for your heart, you need to make choices that will replace the negatives in your life with new positives. God created you and loves you. He has a plan for you, and he will guide you through this time.

Respond Positively

After you have given your spouse space, a time will eventually come when you and your partner will have contact. He may call to check in, or perhaps one of you will need to call or text the other about an important matter. Or you may have to be in communication because of the children. At this point, your response can make a big difference in what happens down the road. Positive instead of negative words can move your relationship in a better direction.

Feeling angry and upset comes naturally in this kind of situation, and if you have expressed such feelings, it's understandable and not surprising. But muster up the resolve to use your words more productively from this time on. Do not hang on to regret and self-incrimination but forgive yourself and move on with a determination to change your reactions. Give everything to God and ask him to calm your heart and emotions so you can have a more upbeat response the next time.

The Bible repeatedly highlights the importance of guarding the mouth and choosing words carefully. Proverbs 21:23 says, "Those who guard their mouths and their tongues keep themselves from calamity," reminding us that "a gentle answer turns away wrath, but a harsh word stirs up anger" (Proverbs 15:1).

Beginning to make encouraging comments on a regular basis can cause your spouse to rethink what she's doing and open up the lines of communication. Offering encouragement may seem contrary to what feels natural to do right now, and it is. Consequently, for this important assignment, you need to continually build up your spiritual muscles by going back to God again and again to receive emotional and spiritual strength.

It may seem impossible to think of positive words to say to mates who have left. If you are struggling with speaking kindly to your separated spouse, sit down and make a list of encouraging comments you could honestly express that would meet your partner's emotional needs. Chapter 4 discusses specifics about how to encourage a spouse in the most effective way. Sometimes even the simplest remarks can have a positive effect. But your words must be sincere. Then pray Psalm 141:3 back to God, "Set a guard over my mouth, LORD; keep watch over the door of my lips." If you ask God to help you with your tongue, he will give you the strength, wisdom, and even the desire to speak words of life into your marriage.

Show, Don't Tell

If you have given your spouse time and space—and if you are focusing on God and nurturing your own growth—you will begin to see yourself changing for the better. When this happens, you may be tempted to point out these successes to your spouse as you go along. However, if you are genuinely changing, your partner will begin to see it when she is around you. Don't tell your partner you are changing; show her. And don't expect to receive any kind of appreciation from her for the next few months. Your mate will hopefully see a new you emerge, but she will probably wonder at first if the changes are real or if you're just making a temporary show to win her back.

Pray

Praying fervently for your spouse is vitally important. But don't merely pray you'll be reconciled. Also pray that your spouse will know God's redemptive grace and become truly committed to him. If husbands or wives have wandered away from God, they probably need to first have a heartfelt experience with Christ before becoming completely committed to their partners again.

Pray for yourself as well, that God will reveal any changes he wants you to make. Regardless of what has transpired in your marriage, each of you has played a part in the brokenness that has taken place. Let God show you how he wants to use the troubles in your marriage to refine your character. Chapter 7 will focus more on how to pray for your marriage.

Surround Yourself with Supportive People

During a separation or other marital crisis, you must choose carefully with whom to share your situation. If you are working to restore your marriage, make sure you have people around you who support your desire to reconcile. Find friends who will listen and not judge, friends who encourage you to look to God for the answers and wait on him.

Often friends do not know what to say. The troubles in your marriage may seem overwhelming to them. If they have not had a personal experience of reconciliation themselves—or know someone who has—they may have a hard time seeing how reconciliation can occur. They care for you, and they want you to be happy. As a result, many of them will tell you, "You don't deserve this," or "You're too good for your husband or wife," or "You can do better." They may encourage you to "get on with your life." These friends want to help. They want you to be happy. What they don't realize is their words may be encouraging you in the wrong direction. Inadvertently, they may be discouraging the marriage and pushing you toward divorce.

TRUST GOD FOR WHAT HAPPENS NEXT

As you work through these principles, you may begin to see your relationship turn around. The change probably will not be a magical moment when everything comes together all at once, but a slow, steady evolution where you begin to experience positive conversations and/or positive times together. Nourish these moments. Discover new and more positive ways to interact with your spouse. Identify things that haven't worked in the past and discard them. Approach this time of separation as an opportunity to build something better between the two of you. Realize also your separation provides the potential for growing into a better and stronger you.

HEART WORK

1. List four specific things you plan to do regularly that will help you take your focus off your spouse. Try to come up with specific church services or Bible studies you plan to attend, teachers you will follow in the media, Christian music to encourage you, books you want to read, ministries to help with, etcetera.

2. What is an activity you enjoy that you can start doing again to nurture yourself without taking on too much of an expense?

3. Make a list of positive things you can say to your spouse to meet his or her emotional needs so you are not at a loss the next time you speak. Be sure whatever you plan to say is sincere. If you have a hard time doing this because of the negativity of recent history, you can even go back to the past and reminisce a little. Just make sure it does not sound like a "why aren't you like that anymore?" remark.

4. Write down the names of at least two people of the same sex who will be supportive of your desire to reconcile with your spouse. Then give yourself a deadline as to when you will try to contact these people and get together with them.

Chapter 2

Sizing Up
Your Relationship Dynamics

We have been separated for several months. This all happened out of the blue. I always thought we were happily married. Our sons and daughter thought life was great. They never saw their mom unhappy for one minute. We never fought. If we had a disagreement we went our own way and it seemed to go away. Now I am finding out my wife was holding in all her anger. She never let anyone know there was something bothering her. She says she loves me but not how I want her to love me. Not like a wife should love a husband. Twenty-nine years and we find ourselves in this situation. It's surreal to me. — *Duane*

Why? Why does something like this happen? And what do you do about it? Is it too late to fight for and save the marriage? As you step back from your circumstances to take a new look at what has been taking place, you may see relationship dynamics in your marriage that were always present but of which you were previously unaware.

How do spouses come to the point, after several years of marriage, where they walk out the door and say it's over? Oftentimes, like Duane above, the forsaken spouse is caught totally by surprise and did not see the separation coming. What happened?

At a Christian bookseller's trade show, I met Chuck. He was a salesman at one of the publisher's booths, and as I perused their new booklist, he asked if he could help. When I told him I was the author of *Broken Heart on Hold, Surviving Separation* and described the book to him, he asked if I had a few minutes to talk. He explained that he and his wife were not living in separate residences but were separated within their own house. She wanted a divorce. He described a number of efforts he had made to try to reconcile, but nothing worked. He did not know what to do.

"I don't know if this applies to you," I said, "but one observation I've made with a number of couples at a marital impasse is that often when a separation occurs, one spouse is more assertive and one spouse is more passive, and it is usually the more passive spouse who wants to leave." I explained a little more what I meant by assertive and passive, and I still remember the stunned look on his face.

"That sounds like our situation," he said. "My wife is the passive one. She doesn't tell me what she's thinking, and I can be pretty persistent at times." After we talked for a while, he left with my book in one hand and a list of changes he was prepared to make in the other. When he emailed me a couple of months later, he saw glimpses of hope.

This is one of many conversations I have had either face-to-face or by email in which people who have been left have a lightbulb moment when I talk about how the passive/assertive issue can affect the marriage relationship. Suddenly, they see a negative undercurrent in their marriage that had been undermining their relationship for years, an undercurrent that finally swept their marriage into the chaos of brokenness. There are many factors that can contribute to the breakdown of a marriage, but if your spouse has left or wants a divorce, prayerfully consider whether the passive/assertive dynamics in your relationship have been partly to blame. As a good soldier walking into battle, the first thing you need to do, as a spouse who wants to rebuild a marriage, is make sure you have clear vision so you can strategically size up the struggle in which you're engaged.

DEGREES OF ASSERTIVENESS AND PASSIVITY

To understand how assertiveness and passivity can affect a marriage, it is important to understand the wide spectrum implied in these terms and in this context. Neither is necessarily wrong, and in most cases, both partners probably need to make adjustments in their relational skills for the marriage to be successful. But if just one spouse is aware of the problem, that person can start the process of change to bring healing.

The words *assertive* and *passive* undoubtedly conjure up a variety of impressions in people's minds. The important thing to consider is the degree of assertiveness and passivity that reigns in the marriage.

Passive spouses may be reluctant to express contrary feelings, or they may not like conflict. They may suppress their own thoughts and feelings to go along with their mate. Passive spouses may be people who try to express their emotions, but they feel inadequate in verbal skills. The passive spouse may be a woman whose understanding of submission has led her to become a doormat. Or the passive one may be a spouse who genuinely feels intimidated by the other, even afraid.

Assertive partners might just be honestly expressing themselves without meaning to shut out the other person. They may be pretty sure of their opinions, but they might be a bit too controlling so their partner never wins arguments and feels powerless. Sometimes, assertive spouses are husbands or wives who are overbearing in their expectations without giving their spouse the freedom to disagree or have different opinions and feelings. Other times, assertive spouses hover and do not give the other the opportunity to have different interests and take time for themselves. Assertive spouses can be people who bulldoze their spouses by pressing their point over and over relentlessly until the worn-out one finally caves. Or an assertive spouse may actually be abusive in words or actions by saying insulting things or using physical force.

A common phenomenon often seen today is the walkaway wife, a woman who packs up and leaves her husband after many years of feeling she has no power in the marriage. Since her husband had no idea there was even a problem, he asks if they can talk about it. Her response?

"For twenty some years I've been trying to talk about it, and you wouldn't listen. Now I'm done."

Whatever the dynamic taking place in the marriage, passive spouses who have not been expressing their needs and wants or who have been expressing them to deaf ears finally get to a point in which they feel suffocated and decide they have had enough. They want to escape, and so the passive spouses leave.

In the book *Boundaries in Marriage*, authors Henry Cloud and John Townsend talk about a love triangle. The triangle consists of freedom, responsibility, and love. For love to thrive they say each person needs to give freedom to their partner. At the same time, a spouse who is feeling crowded in the relationship needs to take responsibility for expressing their own individual needs. Cloud and Townsend write, "Where there is no freedom, there is slavery, and where there is slavery, there will be rebellion. Also, where there is no responsibility, there is bondage. . . . Love can only exist where freedom and responsibility are operating."[1]

WHAT CAN AN ASSERTIVE SPOUSE DO?

If you are the assertive spouse, your first step should be to take the pressure off and begin giving your partner lots of space. If the passive spouse initiated the separation, this includes not calling, texting, or emailing for a period of time. By leaving, the passive spouse has acted out a desire to escape and should be given a chance to breathe.

Meanwhile, if you are the assertive partner, take the opportunity to go to the Lord and ask him to reveal to you the truth about yourself and how you may have been insensitive to your mate. Do not deny the truth. Do not try to defend yourself. Look at yourself squarely in the mirror of Scripture and repent of anything that has taken freedom from your partner. It is possible you have acted unknowingly, figuring you were right and your spouse should just appreciate your good judgment. You did not intend to stifle your mate. But once you see the truth, ask God to forgive you and show you how to change. Then accept his forgiveness. You may do a little grieving over past mistakes, but do not let it stop you from seeking healthier ways of relating. Move forward with God and let him show you the changes you need to make. The Bible clearly shows believers the path to a clean heart: "If we confess our sins, He is faithful and just to forgive us our sins and to cleanse us from all unrighteousness" (1 John 1:9 NKJV).

Once you understand how you need to change and begin implementing new behaviors, ask your partner for forgiveness, but do not try to convince your spouse of your transformation. Let her *see* your changed behavior. In fact, try committing six months to give your spouse space and encouragement without expecting anything from her—no recognition that you are changing, no affirmation, no hugs, nothing. In the meantime, if you are separated, each time you have contact with your mate, say something positive. If you are living in the same house, say one or two positive things each day that builds her up emotionally, and hold your tongue whenever you want to say something negative. Continue to work on yourself and your own issues. Be teachable, and let other people speak honestly to you and help you see your flaws.

In the first email I received from Ron, he told me he did not know where to turn for help. He was separated and hurting. I told him some of the things about assertive and passive spouses, and a month later, I received another email from Ron as he began to see his part in his marriage collapse.

"I needed to change me," he said. "Many things that you bring up are me. Changes were overdue. I wouldn't say I was overly forceful, but I was in my opinions. I had a tendency to wear her down. I know I did that. I would beat an ideal or my opinion about something almost to death at times." As Ron was honest with himself and began focusing on God, he started to change. About sixteen months after they separated, I received an email from Ron and his wife telling me they were reconciling. He now tries to help others who are separated or going through similar situations.

WHAT CAN A PASSIVE SPOUSE DO?

What about passive spouses? What can they do to rescue their marriages? Is it hopeless for them? They probably feel it is. But it's not.

First of all, if you are the passive spouse, begin to speak up. Express your needs, wants, and opinions. Do not expect your spouse to understand your concerns. Years ago, I attended a marriage conference at church. As the counselor spoke about the need to express what we want from our spouse, a friend of mine raised her hand.

"If he really loves me, he should just know what I need and want," she said confidently.

At the time, I inwardly nodded in agreement. *Yes*, I thought. *If he really loves me, he should know.* The naïveté of young love! How dangerous those expectations can be to our marriages! No, your spouse doesn't know how you feel. You need to get past those unrealistic expectations and speak up.

It is your responsibility to tell your mate what you need. If you are feeling overwhelmed in a particular exchange, take a break by excusing yourself to go somewhere to pray and ask God for clarity of thought. Building up spiritual muscle through prayer and asking God for courage will prevent fear or intimidation from shutting you down. You might start by confessing to your husband or wife the realization that you have made a mistake by failing to express yourself in the past. Then let your partner know you want to correct that by sharing what is on your mind. This might actually bring a receptive response. If your spouse is resistant and uncooperative, you may need to seek counsel from a counselor, pastor, or Christian friend to help you find a better way to set up guardrails of protection about your heart while you face your fears and learn to confidently speak "the truth in love" (Ephesians 4:15).

If you are in a situation of being physically abused, however, the above advice is not for you at this time. Read chapter 11 and notify a professional who can help you relocate to a safer situation.

FINDING THE LOVE AGAIN

Understanding where each person fits in this equation can help couples work through stalemates and crisis to find renewed love and fulfillment. Some individuals are more assertive in expressing wishes and opinions; others are more passive or less able to articulate what is on their minds. Reflecting on your relationship to recognize your strengths and weaknesses can help you understand if you may need to offer more freedom to your spouse or if you need to ramp up your courage and begin speaking up. By tempering your own assertiveness or bolstering a new boldness in your conversation, you may begin mending those broken bridges to love.

The Bible tells husbands and wives to have mutual respect for one another. First Peter 3:7 tells husbands, "Husbands, in the same way be considerate as you live with your wives, and treat them with respect as the weaker partner and as heirs with you of the gracious gift of life, so that nothing will hinder your prayers." Ephesians 5:33 tells wives, "the wife must respect her husband."

Neither is to lord it over the other, be bossy, or controlling. Husbands and wives are to respect each other. In marriage, a lack of respect shuts down feelings of love. Understanding how to show appropriate respect for a spouse is often a learning process, requiring an open heart and mind that is attuned to God's Word and responsive to each other's needs.

HEART WORK

1. After reading the above, how would you assess the relationship dynamics in your marriage?

2. Where do you see yourself on a scale of passivity and assertiveness?

3. Spend time in prayer and the mirror of God's Word, asking God to help you see yourself more clearly with your own eyes. Psalm 139:23–24 may help you begin the process.

4. If you are the more assertive one, what steps can you take to give your spouse more freedom?

5. If you are the more passive one, what steps can you make to take more responsibility in getting your concerns heard?

Chapter 3

Exchanging Negative Communication Patterns for Positive Ones

I think it took a lot of time for me to see my part in our problems. Now I guess I need patience to wait for my husband's heart to be open. He is still taking the stance that he is the good guy and all the problems are because of me. — *Denise*

As you load new weapons into your arsenal, you must begin unloading the old ones, the old habits, the old rebuttals, the old defenses and excuses—the ones you may have relied on, usually subconsciously. Often we resist making changes because it's the way we have learned to cope. It's "the way we are." We do and say what comes naturally. We must remember, however, we are all sinful, fallen creatures, and what comes naturally may need to undergo the scalpel of God's surgical but merciful removal so we can submit to the transformation he wants to make in us.

During one of the hardest points of Marv's and my three-year separation, I was desperate for answers.

Brokenhearted and not knowing what to do, I went to a pastoral counselor at our church who said, "When couples come to me talking about divorce, I find they don't really want to divorce the *person* in the marriage; they want to divorce the *form* of the marriage." I quizzed him about this, but he did not explain further. From that time on, his words continued to haunt me. I was intrigued. What did he mean by the *form* of the marriage? How could I change the form of my marriage? With those questions swirling in my head, I began my own private search for answers.

My quest began by reading books, studying Scripture, praying for understanding, and listening intently to those who were wiser than I, including pastors and Christian friends. I even asked my daughters and family members for honest assessments of my character flaws.

Gradually, I began to uncover a basic misconception that many people have when their marriages hit the wall. Even though the marriage is in crisis, spouses tend to keep maneuvering within the same patterns of interaction that have shaped their marriages all along, reacting to one another in the same old familiar ways. But since those old patterns were not working for Marv and me, I began to realize that in our marriage those old communication and behavior patterns were part of the problem. We needed to do something different. But what?

INTERRUPTING THOSE NEGATIVE REACTIONARY CIRCLES

Early in our marriage, when Marv and I drove through Europe, we frequently found ourselves caught up on rotary traffic circles in the cities. Looping about a city landmark on the inner part of a multi-lane traffic circle, we would struggle in vain to get into the outer lane in time to turn onto the intersecting street that would continue us on our way. Without fail, we would be unable to break into the heavy stream of oncoming cars, and we missed our turn. Consequently, it usually meant many lost minutes as we drove round and round the traffic circle in a seemingly futile effort to get to our destination.

The same kind of thing often happens in marriages. As spouses respond to one another, they form reactionary circles that take them around and around in a repetitive pattern of interaction as certain words, actions, or gestures from each other propel them into a predictable pattern of exchanges. Spouses can go round and round with the same negative retorts, emotional outbursts, actions, excuses, or silences that produce the same frustration and hurts. When the episode is over, each partner may not even know what happened. All they know is one or both spouses are hurt and angry with the other, once again. Each partner may feel helpless to make things different. They may think, *If only he would change.*

The good news is either spouse can interrupt the sequence of interactions that make up these circular communication blockages. If you are working toward a healthier marriage, every exchange that takes place between you and your partner can either maintain the pattern as it is or redefine it. If you choose to alter your own responses noticeably and consistently, your mate's reactions will change, which will in turn cause you to react in a different way toward him or her. In this way, you can intentionally cause a destructive communication cycle to spin out in a new, more positive direction.

Here is a scenario that could very well play out in a number of homes:

Betty: You always do that!
Don: No, I don't. You always blame me for everything!
Betty: I don't blame you for everything. You never admit it when you do something wrong!
Don: Well, according to you, I never do anything right!
Betty: You're changing the subject.
Don: I'm tired of being blamed for everything.

At any point during this exchange, either Betty or Don could have responded differently and turned the dialogue in a different, more constructive direction. Proverbs 15:23 says, "A person finds joy in giving an apt reply—and how good is a timely word!"

Here are some approaches you can use to interrupt a negative reactionary circle:

• Pause to listen instead of reacting immediately. And really listen!
• Accept and validate your spouse's feelings and experience.

- Use words of encouragement, acceptance, trust, understanding, and reassurance.
- Be aware of negative facial expressions, tone of voice, and body language.
- Be a team. Use "I" statements rather than blaming, e.g., "If only you would . . . "
- Find ways to laugh at yourself or use humor (not sarcasm) in an awkward moment.
- Consider whether or not your mate has a valid point, and affirm his or her right to make it by rephrasing it back to them.
- In hostile situations, stop and pray before reacting.

Each conversation with your spouse can potentially steer things in a new direction. Even careful listening sends a message as you interpret his words in negative or positive ways. If you are misinterpreting what he says, your response will reflect that misunderstanding and create a new kink in the communication process.

On the other hand, if you consciously choose your words and responses, one small change can have a happy ripple effect that not only allows the marital dynamics to change but gradually restores the positive feelings of love and respect between husband and wife.

During a marital separation, if contact is limited, try to make the most of each encounter. When something negative arises, pray about it and ask God to show you a positive way to respond so those normal reactionary cycles are interrupted and a new path to understanding can open.

THINKING IT THROUGH

Hopefully, this list has teased your mind about how to interrupt the negative reactionary circles taking place in your marriage, but these approaches deserve further exploration to see how you might apply them. Chapter 4 will delve more carefully into how to use encouragement to break a destructive communication cycle, and chapter 14 will talk more about the use of "I" statements. Chapters 7 and 10 dive deeply into the world of prayer to better understand how to pray for a marriage. So let's look at the other items on this list.

Are You Listening?

A common problem in many marriages involves the process of speaking and listening. I love the folksy saying of Joe Williams, coauthor of *Yes, Your Marriage Can Be Saved* and cofounder of Marriage 911: "God gave us two ears and one mouth so we would listen more and talk less."[1] Unfortunately, too many of us use our mouths too much and allow our ears to pick up only what they want to hear.

Psychologists say when one person speaks to another, three different messages actually occur simultaneously:

1. What the person intends to say
2. What is actually said
3. What the other person hears

What we hear is more than a physical act as we ascribe our own meaning to the words and incorporate the subtle nuances we see and hear in tone of voice, facial expressions, and body language. Sometimes our insecurities or prejudices lend incorrect interpretations to what our spouse is actually saying. Other times, we are not really listening but thinking of how we can offer a good rebuttal to what we think the other is saying. By asking God for wisdom and patience in our interactions, we can hear each other's concerns and hopefully understand each other's hearts. James 1:19–20 says, "My dear brothers and sisters, take note of this: Everyone should be quick to listen, slow to speak and slow to become angry, because human anger does not produce the righteousness that God desires." In short, the Bible says to listen more and talk less.

Validating Your Spouse's Feelings

When Jane first came to the Marriage 911 class my husband and I lead, she was deeply depressed because her husband would not come with her or even recognize that their marriage needed help. When Jane told her husband she was depressed about what was happening in their relationship, he became defensive and blamed her for their problems.

He refused to acknowledge her emotions. As a result, their communication collapsed into a period of bankruptcy.

Another person's emotions can sometimes feel threatening, particularly if that someone is a spouse. If you don't know how to help her feel better, you may find it easier to simply deny that her emotions are genuine. And then you may try to fix her.

I remember as a teen trying to engage my mother with some common teenage complaints, expressing to her that I felt left out, not good enough or not pretty enough, and she would respond with, "You shouldn't feel that way, Linda." And then she would tell me why I should not feel that way. Of course, she just wanted to help. She didn't want me to feel bad. In fact, she probably honestly felt I had no reason to feel bad. But I did, and without a listening ear, those negative feelings had no place to go except deep down inside where I had to struggle with them by myself. The same dynamic can take place between spouses.

Our experiences and feelings are our own. Telling someone not to feel a certain way negates very legitimate feelings. Feelings are not right or wrong. We feel what we feel. Accepting and validating your spouse's feelings and experiences provides a sense of safety, promotes communication, and helps the healing process so your partner can get beyond those emotions and move on more positively.

Recognizing Negative Body Language

I once visited at a couple's house after the husband had just had knee surgery. The wife was dutifully preparing a compress for his knee. When he asked her a question, she responded with the right words, but the tone of her voice and the expression on her face showed irritation. I wondered what message the husband was receiving. She was doing something loving, but the undertones of her message showed irritation. Did he feel loved or unloved? Did he feel cared for? Or did he feel he was a burden?

We seldom realize how our facial expressions, tone of voice, or body language is contradicting or undermining what our words are saying to our spouse. Only when we consciously stop to think about it can we make adjustments so we accurately communicate what we intend to say.

Thinking as a Team

In my quest for truth during my husband's and my separation, God opened my eyes a little at a time to see ways he wanted to change me and my responses to my husband. Thinking of my husband and me as a team was an important first step. If God made us to be "one" in marriage (Matthew 19:5), it makes sense for us to join together as a team in our problem solving and decision-making. One of the first times I had a chance to apply this new concept was when I received something in the mail that had negative financial repercussions. In my normal fleshly way of reacting, I would have called my husband with a sense of righteous indignation and laid the blame at his feet. This time, however, I prayed about it first, allowed God's peace to settle over me, and called my husband with the words, "I think we have a problem." I explained the situation calmly, and he responded thoughtfully with a plan of action. The next time we talked, I noticed he had a gentler and less defensive attitude.

Ephesians 4:23–24 tells us, "To be made new in the attitude of [our] minds; and to put on the new self, created to be like God in true righteousness and holiness." Learning to think of my husband and me as a team instead of adversaries where one of us had to be at fault brought about a restructuring in my approach to problems. On a football team when one player messes up, other players jump in to grab the ball and run with it. Similarly, spouses are more apt to win the game when they act as a team. For Marv and me, it was a small beginning in turning our relationship in a new direction.

Using Humor

The Proverbs 31 woman is regarded by Christians as the ideal woman. One of her strengths is she can laugh in the face of uncertain circumstances. "She is clothed with strength and dignity; she can laugh at the days to come. She speaks with wisdom, and faithful instruction is on her tongue" (Proverbs 31:25–26). What gives her this ability to laugh? I believe it is the confidence and security she has in knowing God will take care of her no matter what the future holds.

I love this added dimension to her character. Not only is the Proverbs 31 woman wise, strong, confident, and dignified but she has a sense of humor. A lot of us could benefit from adding laughter to our arsenal of weapons to fight off the sting of conflict and disappointment. Having a healthy sense of humor can help us put life's circumstances in perspective. Occasionally, seeing the funny side of a situation can defuse the tension and help us lighten up a little. Life's troubles and a spouse's frailties may pale a bit and not appear as huge a problem as we first thought.

Sarcasm, however, is not a positive use of humor when it comes to relationships. Although it may feel good to the initiator, its effect is usually to tear down the other person. A healthy use of humor will allow both spouses to laugh.

Clarifying What You Hear

Even before the words come out of your partner's mouth, there may be times when you've already formed a negative or skewed opinion about the point of view he is trying to express. To help you hear your mate correctly, instead of interpreting his words according to your own assumptions, prejudices, or insecurities, it sometimes helps to rephrase it back, particularly if what he's said seems unclear or strikes you negatively.

To check out your understanding of what your spouse has said, try rephrasing it back to him: "What I hear you saying is. . . . Is that right?" If your spouse says no, ask to hear it again. If he says yes and you want to score extra points, you might even want to say, "Hmm, tell me more about that."

This technique has helped many couples work through some sticky issues in their relationships. Certain therapists use it in their counseling to facilitate a clearer understanding between husband and wife and open up better pathways of communication. A woman, who later became a counselor, touted this technique as being instrumental in saving her marriage years earlier.

ALLOWING GOD TO DO HIS TRANSFORMING WORK

I believe God uses these troubling times in our lives to build up the unique qualities he saw in us when he first molded us in our mothers' wombs and spoke our names into existence. He wants us to be strong and glorify him. As we come to him, he will show us the changes he wants us to make to become all he created us to be.

Scripture often uses the marriage relationship as an allegory for the relationship between God and his people. Consequently, I believe marriage is a natural place for God to begin transforming us into the uniquely special people he first envisioned us to be. Romans 12:2 says, "Do not conform to the pattern of this world, but be transformed by the renewing of your mind. Then you will be able to test and approve what God's will is—his good, pleasing and perfect will." Actively changing disagreeable patterns in your marriage can open doors to God's healing. Your crisis can actually become a time of growth, a time for God's refining fire to burn away some of the chaff so both you and your spouse can become the people he designed.

When my husband and I reconciled in 1998, we had become more sensitive to each other's needs. My husband willingly began to confront problems with me and took more responsibility around the house, and I learned to approach problems as a team player and give him the appreciation he needed as a man.

God knows each marriage is made up of two fallible human beings. His hope is that we will turn to him so he can use the impossibilities within our marriages to change us and fit us into the possibilities of his greater plan.

HEART WORK

1. Can you identify some negative reactionary circles that have consistently taken place in your marriage? Take time to pray about this, and then list them below.

    1.

    2.

    3.

2. How can you choose to respond differently in each of the above circumstances?

3. Look at yourself in the mirror when you are upset with your mate. Talk to yourself as if talking to him or her, and watch your expression. Could your facial expressions, tone of voice, or body language be sending an unwanted message? Pray about this and ask God to show you how to make necessary changes.

4. When your spouse starts sharing an idea that seems impractical or unrealistic in some way or shares negative feelings, how do you react? Do you listen and let your partner finish explaining? Or do you try to fix the situation or respond in a critical manner?

5. When you are in an argument and your partner is talking, are you listening to his or her words, reacting to the emotion you see behind the words, or thinking about what you want to say?

6. How can you insert humor into your exchanges?

Chapter 4

Finding Power
in Positive Words

Yesterday afternoon, I was frustrated and called my husband a bad word. Please pray for me that I don't say things when I get frustrated. It only complicates things. I miss doing things with him like going for a walk or bike ride. When I asked him to go with me, he replied, "You could go by yourself." I should have left it alone, but I didn't. Please pray I don't say or do things I might regret later. — *Edith*

At the end of each marriage class Marv and I lead, I always hand out a coffee filter to the women in my small group. Not because we're going to make coffee but because of a story I tell during the class that has become a favorite. In fact, some of those who succeed in reconciling seemingly hopeless marriages tell me this story is one of the key reasons they were able to fully pull their marriages back together.

The story comes from Nancy C. Anderson and her book *Avoiding the Greener Grass Syndrome*. She calls it the Parable of the Coffee Filter.[1] I will paraphrase it here in my own words as I do when I tell the story in class.

As a wife, Nancy admits she had nagged and controlled. Even her brother scolded her for being so critical of her husband. Soon after one of her brother's visits, Nancy began to feel convicted about how she interacted with her husband. She went to the kitchen to make coffee and remembered the day she forgot to put in the coffee filter. When the coffee flowed into the pot, it was bitter, yucky, and full of grounds—totally undrinkable. In that moment, it was like a neon sign flashing a picture before her of what her words were like when she said whatever came to mind without filtering it first. Like the unfiltered coffee, her words were bitter, yucky, and coarse.

Memories of certain Scriptures came to Nancy's mind: "A nagging wife annoys like constant dripping" (Proverbs 19:13 TLB), and "Put a guard over my mouth that I may not sin with it" (Psalm 141:3 paraphrase).

Humbled by this new revelation, she prayed, "Oh, please, Lord, install a filter between my brain and my mouth. Help me to choose my words carefully. I want my speech to be smooth and mellow."

Like Nancy, so many of us spout off whatever comes into our minds without first filtering the words. As a result, words can often be hurtful, ugly, demeaning, critical, caustic, overbearing, sarcastic, or demanding.

As we practice putting that filter in our minds, we will begin to recognize words that need to be filtered out and block them before they are spoken. Using that coffee filter may also awaken a deeper truth. If we are asking God to help tame our language, he may begin to show us there is more to this than just our words. That is what happened to me.

A HEART ISSUE

One day, in the midst of the three years my husband and I were separated, God pruned my heart when I ran across the following words from Jesus,

> For out of the abundance of the heart the mouth speaks. The good person brings good things out of a good treasure, and the evil person brings evil things out of an evil treasure. I tell you, on the day of judgment you will have to give an account for every careless word you utter; for by your words you will be justified, and by your words you will be condemned." (Matthew 12:34b–37 NRSV)

The passage hit me hard. I suddenly saw that the critical and sometimes sarcastic remarks that came from my lips had deeper roots than mere words alone. And I was mortified at the revelation. My negative words and attitudes came from my heart.

So, what was wrong with my heart?

For the next year, I went through my Bible, studying all the references to the heart, trying to digest what God wanted to say to me. As a result, God used this painful time of separation from my husband to circumcise my heart and refine the words that overflowed from it.

Because of this, even before my husband and I began to reconcile, I started to see changes in my reactions to him. The Holy Spirit was making me new. Although unnatural for me in my worldly nature, new, softer responses began to flow from my lips naturally. While negative reactions and thoughts still popped up in my mind, surprisingly, the words came out of my mouth in a more thoughtful, gentle way.

A NEW HUMILITY

When Ellen came to our class, she was very critical of her husband. In her mind, he was responsible for all of their problems. Just a couple of weeks into the program, the assignment was to write down all the positive qualities about the spouse. Ellen came to our group the next week almost in tears, telling us how she realized what a good man he really was and how she and her negative words were responsible for many of their problems.

From that moment, Ellen truly became a different person. Her face and demeanor lit up with a new attractiveness. She talked about using the coffee filter often and even spoke about it with her children. One evening, she told the story of how her son had interrupted her when Ellen was going on and on about something that had just happened.

"Mommy," he said. Her son circled his fingers around the top of his head like a filter. Ellen laughed. Even her family had begun to appreciate the Parable of the Coffee Filter.

Humbling ourselves before God, asking him to give us more careful, positive responses and visualizing that coffee filter in our brains can help our thoughts swirl around in our heads before we utter them, allowing our words to come out smooth and rich instead.

The first part of finding the power of positive words is to allow God to cleanse your heart so you can learn to subdue the negative ones. When your heart is purified, God can teach you to communicate in ways that nurture your marital relationship instead of stifling it. If you are fighting to reconcile with your spouse, the Parable of the Coffee Filter may help you reflect on your words before you speak them. That brief respite gives God a chance to soothe your mind with his peace so the words can take on a gentler tone. Then, with a fresh and humble heart, new words will start to take their place.

POSITIVE WORDS

The importance of words, however, goes beyond simply restraining the negative ones. Positive words have power. Proverbs 18:21 says "death and life are in the power of the tongue" (NASB). Just as negative words can bring death—even to a marriage—positive ones can result in life. Words have power. They can hurt and they can heal. Proverbs 16:24 says, "Pleasant words are a honeycomb, Sweet to the soul and healing to the bones" (NASB). Speaking positive words consistently can change the dynamics of a marriage.

IDENTIFYING INDIVIDUAL NEEDS

Early in my husband's and my separation, I not only realized how my negative words had hurt our marriage, but by reading marriage books and applying them to our fractured relationship, I became more sensitive to my husband's needs and my deficiency in responding to them. Although I tried to be kind and thoughtful in my conversation, I began to understand that a relationship requires not only kindness and thoughtfulness, but also words that express sensitivity to the person's specific needs. Consequently, I started to recognize that my husband needed more affirmation from me. He needed my approval—even my admiration at times—to fuel the love reservoir that kept our relationship alive.

As I thought back on our early marriage, I knew these were the kinds of words I had given him back then. What changed? It was a slow unraveling, and I believe the same downhill slide that happened to us occurs in many other marriages as well.

During the demands of everyday family life, verbal exchanges can easily shift from fostering a relationship to fostering a routine. You may lose sense of your spouse's personal needs and focus on responsibilities instead. Your mate becomes your partner in solving problems and fulfilling responsibilities rather than a person who needs the appreciation you may have lavished on her when you were dating or first married.

If you want to begin speaking encouraging words to your spouse, you may first need to reacquaint yourself with who your spouse actually is. Pray that you can start to see your partner through God's eyes as you sit down with a pad of paper and think about:

- What makes your spouse happy, sad, or angry?
- What makes your partner hopeful or discouraged?
- What are your spouse's strengths?
- What makes your mate feel loved and appreciated?
- What is your spouse afraid of?
- What is your partner most proud of?
- Where is your spouse afraid of failing?

A spouse who has left is undoubtedly feeling an emotional disconnect from you. His or her reservoir of love may have been depleted and needs to be replenished. So now that your marriage has hit this bitter place, how might encouraging words help the two of you reestablish an emotional connection? Ephesians 4:29 asks believers to build "others up according to their needs." Pray about how you can pour words of love into your spouse's hurts, bolster his strengths and affirm her as an individual.

In his letters to the Corinthians, Romans, and Ephesians, Paul talks frequently about the importance of love, and he describes what it looks like to love. These are some of the phrases Paul uses:

- "Accept one another" (Romans 15:7)
- "Build him up" (Romans 15:2)

- "Be devoted, . . . honor one another" (Romans 12:10)
- "Be completely humble and gentle; be patient, bearing with one another in love" (Ephesians 4:2)
- "Be kind and compassionate, forgiving each other" (Ephesians 4:32)
- "Always protects, always trusts, always hopes, and always perseveres" (1 Corinthians 13:7)
- "Do not be proud, rude, self-seeking or easily angered" (1 Corinthians 13:4–5)

LOOKING AT DIFFERENCES

As you plumb the depths of your spouse's needs, you should also consider how your spouse differs from you. What builds you up may not be the same as what builds up your partner. Consider your different personality types, love languages, and genders.

In terms of differences between men and women, we may want to take a cue from Scripture, which emphasizes the need for men to love their wives and women to respect their husbands. In knitting together the man and woman, God seems to have wired differences in their emotional needs as well. Both need love and respect, but the proportion of each that men and women require and how their love needs are satisfied may not be the same. In fact, scientific studies of the brain now show that men and women's brains have different emotional responses.[2]

Pondering your spouse's needs and Paul's principles of showing love, how can you speak encouraging words into the life of your spouse?

SHOWING ENCOURAGEMENT DURING YOUR SEPARATION

If you are still living in the same house, working together, or regularly interacting with your spouse because of the children, you have more opportunity to speak positive words. But if you seldom see each other, you will have to wait until you have contact. Each time you interact, be prepared with positive things to say.

When I realized my inattentiveness in not speaking words that conveyed encouragement to my husband, it was an eye-opener. But, honestly, the idea of telling my husband words that showed trust, appreciation, acceptance, and admiration was a tall order during those early days of our separation. Our relationship was extremely tense and distant. He was not doing too much that I felt warranted that kind of encouragement. But I knew building him up and speaking into his emotional needs was key to repairing the damage that had been done to our marriage.

So, I sat down with a pen and paper and listed everything I could think of that he was doing right or things I could appreciate or accept or trust—even things from the past. And then, each time we had contact by phone or in person, I tried to work something from my list into the conversation. Sometimes it was something like: "I know you're doing the best you can;" "I know you'll make the right decision;" "I appreciate you sending me that money;" "I know you want to do the right thing." Other times I reminisced: "You were such a good teacher in that Sunday school class. You could always make people laugh and hold their attention;" "You were a really attentive father in the way you always came to the children's softball games and ballet recitals."

If you are a marriage warrior, a spouse fighting for reconciliation, begin thinking about positive words or actions you can speak into the emotional needs of your spouse. Make a list. Then, take advantage of times you and your spouse are together and be intentional about using them.

How can you apply this in practical ways? Even the simple act of saying words of appreciation like *thank you* can be a positive first step. If you want to show appreciation to your spouse, focus upon the little things she does, such as picking the kids up from school, calling to coordinate the children's calendar, paying a bill, calling to check on you, or telling you about changes at work.

To honor your spouse, let him hear you speak well of him in front of others.

Encouraging comments, such as, *I think that's really great that you*_____ (fill in the blank) will make him feel appreciated.

For both men and women, positive listening and patient silence can be just as important as positive words.

Being patient and kind might involve listening to jumbled up thoughts without trying to correct your spouse or fix the problem. Yes, the answer for your spouse's concerns may be clear to you, but your partner may need to find the answers without your help. Talking without being interrupted may bring needed clarity to her thinking.

If your spouse is complaining about you, really listen. Instead of defending yourself, take a deep breath, nod your head, and say, "Okay, I'll think about that." Then go to the Bible or talk to a Christian friend to see if there is truth to your partner's concerns. If there is, act accordingly. Your spouse may feel validated, understood, and cared for.

To show caring and devotion, let your wife know you are available if she wants to talk or needs something.

If your husband does not express his thoughts to you, show patience, acceptance, and trust by letting him figure things out for himself. When appropriate, you might say, "I know you're confused about what you want right now. Take some time to think it through;" "I know you want to do what's right, and I trust you to find the answers you need."

At one point, I discovered my husband wanted my trust. This was important to him. I cannot say I felt he deserved my trust after having left me, but even if I couldn't trust him with our relationship at the time, there were small things I could trust him with. One day, my husband and I were going to a restaurant across town.

When he headed in a direction that seemed inconsistent with our destination, I asked, "Where are you going?" Obviously offended, he explained his reasons for taking a different route than usual. I hadn't trusted he knew what he was doing, and he needed my trust.

So I found that trusting him with something simple like knowing how to get to our destination or finding a parking place—all by himself—without my trying to help him out by pointing one out for him helped him feel trusted. Sometimes it's hard to just be silent. But at times *no* words are the *best* words. By me demonstrating how I could trust him with minor things, he began to feel more adequate in our relationship and deserving of my forgiveness.

If you are a man whose wife has left, one very important thing you may need to do is really listen to your wife. Validate her feelings. Reassure her about what she is doing or has done right. Be considerate of her needs. If you think she needs assistance with something and you feel comfortable helping, tell her you would be glad to support her, and ask if she wants you to do that. Do not assume. Be respectful by asking. Appreciate her. Compliment her on a new shirt or hairdo. Be available if she needs you to do something. Tell her you understand she needs time to think and you want her to have the time she needs to do that. Each time you have contact, work something positive into the conversation.

If you are a woman whose husband has left, when you talk to your husband, build him up, not in terms of your love for him or your belief in your marriage, but speak about what a special man he is. Tell him how you appreciate his devotion to his children or his careful handling of your finances. Although you may not like everything he is doing, realize trying to change him will have negative rather than positive consequences. Instead, demonstrate acceptance. Show trust in little things whenever you can. Make a list of everything positive you can think of about him, and speak words of encouragement or admiration each time you have contact. Build him up as a man. If he makes a decision you honestly approve of, let him know that. If he is handy about fixing things and you need something repaired around the house, you might let him fix it for you. Fixing a tangible problem for you can make him feel good about himself, and that is good for your relationship.

SHOWING LOVE

Some comments, which you personally would regard as positive, can actually have the opposite effect on a partner who is confused about the marriage. What seems logical to the spouse fighting for the marriage to stay intact may actually be perceived as offensive by the one who wants to leave. If you are the spouse who wants to reconcile, reminding your partner of the good things about your marriage may seem positive to you, but these reminders may feel like accusations to a spouse who wants to separate. Saying, "I love you," may make your spouse feel guilty and defensive if he or she doesn't reciprocate those feelings at this particular time. Under normal circumstances, these words would be positive, but during a separation, the leaving spouse may feel pressured by them and tend to pull away even more.

Consider, instead, showing love by identifying in your spouse what author Gary Chapman calls a love language. According to his book, *The Five Love Languages*, each of us responds more positively to one or two of the love languages described below. During separation, understanding your spouse's love language can be a step toward reviving the relationship. Think about your spouse as you read the following. To which expression of love does your spouse respond?

Quality time[3]—If one spouse has been too busy at work and the other spouse's love language is quality time, the spouse may have felt neglected. If you are separated, making yourself available when your spouse reaches out to you may be a positive step forward.

Gifts[4]—If one spouse anticipates receiving gifts on birthdays, but gift giving has seemed frivolous to the other spouse, the one for whom gift giving is a love language may feel unloved. A thoughtful gift at appropriate times during a separation may create more receptive feelings.

Words of affirmation[5]—Some people need to hear encouraging and affirming words to feel valued. Those whose love language is words of affirmation will be particularly responsive to what this chapter addresses. Hearing positive words may fuel their love tank.

Acts of service[6]— For those whose love language is acts of service, hearing words that aren't backed up by actions can make the words seem superfluous. Being helpful tells them of your love. When actions are not present, they may feel a distance in the relationship. They may not even know why, but their feelings can grow cold as a result. Thoughtful acts of service during a separation may begin to thaw the ice between you.

Physical touch[7]—Some people crave physical touch like hugs or hand holding. If your spouse's love language is physical touch and times together failed to include touching, your spouse may have experienced feelings of rejection. During a separation, demonstrative acts of touch may at this time be unwelcome, but pats on the shoulder and an occasional hug might begin to warm up the relationship.

CREATING SAFETY

If your spouse has left the marriage and you desire reconciliation, consider what it would look like to create safety whenever you interact together. Refrain from talking about your marriage and its problems. Your goal should basically be to offer uplifting words and actions that buoy up your spouse as an individual to make him feel valued. When your spouse feels valued by you, she may feel safer with you and begin to open up to you. Focus on creating a pleasant, enjoyable, and safe environment for the times the two of you are together. One important caveat is that you must not expect anything from your mate in return. Do not expect appreciation, thanks, acknowledgment, hugs, kind words, or smiles. Positive words are simply a gift, not a plea for approval. If you are making changes to save your marriage, let God be the one to bless your heart with his love for the changes you are making. Once your spouse has become more receptive and begins to see positive change in you, there will hopefully come a time when you can talk about your marriage.

If your spouse has left and your heart is broken, some of this advice is probably very difficult to hear. Most likely, you can think of a lot of negative things to say but not too many positive ones. Showing encouragement may go against the grain of your feelings. But if you want things to change—if you want to give your marriage a chance to be restored—you need to allow God to build up your spiritual muscles so you can muster the strength to do what it seems humanly unnatural to do. Romans 15:1 says those "who are strong ought to bear with the failings of the weak." Your spouse may be in a weak place right now. Speaking positive words into your spouse's life can have a powerful effect.

With these various weapons in your arsenal, spend time each day asking God for wisdom in how and when to use them. He has the answers. He can give you strength and discernment to do what is most effective and valuable. If you feel a check in your spirit when you attempt to follow through on the advice from others (even me), listen carefully to the Father's voice.

HEART WORK

1. What kinds of negative words are you guilty of using with your spouse? Spend some time praying and asking God to reveal these to you.

2. Get a coffee filter. Pick out a couple of the following Scriptures and write them on the filter. Then place the coffee filter on your refrigerator or mirror where you will see it often.

    Pleasant words are a honeycomb, Sweet to the soul and healing to the bones. (Proverbs 16:24 NASB)

    The one who guards his mouth preserves his life; The one who opens wide his lips comes to ruin. (Proverbs 13:3 NASB)

    A gentle answer turns away wrath, But a harsh word stirs up anger. (Proverbs 15:1 NASB)

    He who guards his mouth and his tongue, guards his soul from troubles. (Proverbs 21:23 NASB)

    Set a guard, O LORD, over my mouth; Keep watch over the door of my lips. (Psalm 141:3 NASB)

3. Ask God to show you your spouse's strengths, fears, and other emotional needs. Write them down so you can reflect on them. Then, seek God's guidance on how to speak encouragement into your partner's heart.

4. Make a list of your spouse's good qualities and things your partner does or has done that you see as positive. Plan what you will say the next time you have contact.

5. What things can you do that would help your spouse know he/she is loved by you?

Chapter 5

Drawing on Outside Help

We've gone to so many counselors and I think they actually made it worse. One counselor, about the age of my husband, was all buddy-buddy to my husband at the first meeting, talking about their guy stuff as if they were best friends. I was just sitting there—invisible. Then the counselor started asking me confrontational questions, none to him. Shortly I was in tears, sobbing, feeling ganged up on; I left the session, went outside and sat on the curb crying and crying. Neither came to check on me, just left me dying inside. Finally, my husband came out and said the counselor said I was a really bitter woman. We never went back. —*Janine*

Where do you turn for support during a marriage separation? Who can help you through the pain so you can see clearly enough to wade through the confusion?

Those who are separated walk a lonely path and need others in their lives to buoy them up and hold them together. Not knowing where to go for encouragement causes many people to remain isolated during one of the loneliest times of their lives. Others seek help, but like Janine above, they end up more confused and hurt because of feeling misunderstood. Unfortunately, even therapists, if they are unskilled in navigating the complexities of marriage counseling, can harm the marriage more than help it.

If you are separated, you are on a journey you should not take alone. Seeking out constructive support is an important component of fighting for your marriage. This chapter offers advice on what to look for and what to avoid when drawing on help.

You can receive needed support on this journey in various ways. During our three-year separation, at some point Marv and I each took advantage of four of the support systems listed below. All helped us in some manner on the road to our eventual reconciliation:

- Friends or family
- Pastors, lay counselors, and mentors
- Peer programs
- Professional counseling
- Marriage intensives

FRIENDS AND FAMILY

Regardless of how else you receive help when you are separated, friends are an extremely important part of your daily life. It's essential that you choose friends who can be trusted with confidential information and are supportive of marriage reconciliation without trying to tell you what to do. You need people who will mainly listen and provide encouragement without judging you if your actions sometimes seem out of character.

When I interviewed Roger Shepherd on the phone (he's a licensed mental health counselor and senior supervisor of the counseling program at Reformed Theological Seminary), he had a lot to say on this topic. He believes friends help when they're showing up and invested. "I don't mean coming in and telling them what to do but coming in and giving them a safe place to be honest."

Family can provide an important and loving support system during this time. Be sure to take advantage of the comfort they offer, but in your search for confidantes, you may want to be careful about divulging too many of the hurtful details to those who might be prone to judge your spouse too severely. Those who love you and are closest to you may have a harder time forgiving if reconciliation occurs.

PASTORS, LAY COUNSELORS, AND MENTORS

Pastors and lay counselors can be very valuable if, as Robert S. Paul of Focus on the Family said in a phone interview with me, "a lay counselor knows how to be a helper and facilitator as opposed to a director."

At the most intense point of our separation, when my husband first told me he wanted a divorce, I went to our church's counseling pastor. His gentle encouragement challenged me to think about how I could make changes in the dynamics of our marriage. Ultimately, that led me to the realization that reconciliation all began with me making changes in myself. I did not want a divorce, and this pastor's comments gave me hope. Later, my friend Kathy showed up as a friend to accompany me on my journey. Her wisdom and strong Christian faith supported, mentored, and challenged me during that rough time.

Likewise, my husband, Marv, spent time with an evangelist/counselor and his wife. These two helped point him back toward the Lord. Marv and I still had a long way to go, but their tender and caring support steered him in a more positive direction. Later on, when we were closer to reconciling, another friend showed up to mentor my husband and help him take the necessary steps of accountability so trust could be rebuilt in our relationship.

Ultimately, each person on this journey needs to seek God for answers and direction. But laypeople can support you in your search when they come along beside you and speak to you from their own experience and knowledge.

PEER PROGRAMS

For many years, excellent peer programs throughout the country and internationally have offered important help to marriages, including my own.

Retrouvaille

Two and a half years into my husband's and my separation, we thought we would like to reconcile but still had fears about actually doing it. We attended a Retrouvaille weekend, and the program gave us valuable new tools for communicating with each other by helping us connect at a heart level. It gave us the confidence we needed to get back together.

Since that time, we have referred many couples who were able to delve beneath the conflict tearing them apart to find a deeper connection and move toward reconciliation. In the final session of the program, it is amazing to hear couples who came with divorce papers in hand talk about how the program has changed their decision and their lives. Retrouvaille is an international program, usually sponsored by the Catholic Church but welcoming to all faiths. It can be found in almost every state in the United States and in some other countries as well. It is not a spiritual retreat or counseling session, and couples are not asked to share problems with anyone other than their spouse in private settings. The program consists of a weekend and six follow-up sessions. You can find out more at retrouvaille.org.

Marriage 911

For many years, my husband and I have been leaders in Marriage 911, a Christ-centered, life-changing class that takes place, not only in our local area, but in sixty cities across the United States, as well as Canada, Australia, and the Virgin Islands. One of the unique aspects about Marriage 911 is that both partners do not have to attend for it to have a positive impact on the marriage. Even one person who is motivated to see change can make a difference. The course helps each person think through individual motives, responses, and interactions when confronting various issues in their marriage. Marv and I have seen countless marriages restored through the tools and support offered in this twelve- to thirteen-week program developed by Joe and Michelle Williams. For those who do not have Marriage 911 close enough to their place of residence, Joe and Michelle will arrange an online class at a convenient time. You can find out more at http://Marriage911godsway.com.

PROFESSIONAL COUNSELING

When Liz and her husband decided to get back together after a six-year separation, she asked me for recommendations for a counselor. Her husband was an introvert with health issues, and she had abandonment issues that tended to intensify when he pulled away for time alone. After going to the counselor, she sent me an email.

> We did go see Roger, the counselor you recommended, and we were helped with looking into the feelings behind all of our hurtful behavior. We have found that being unaware of our own baggage and focused on the other spouse's broken parts really caused a great deal of pain for both of us. Roger was very helpful. We are living together and working on quality time spent meeting each other's emotional needs. Thank you so much for your prayers. I know the Lord is working in our lives.

Liz's note provides an example of how a good marriage counselor can play an important role in healing a marriage. In choosing a marriage counselor, it's important to start by selecting one with a biblical worldview about the importance of marriage. However, there are other important factors to consider as well. Counselors who are unskilled in marriage counseling can actually undermine or even sabotage the relationship. All therapists are not equal in their ability to help, especially when it comes to marriage counseling.

Bill Doherty, professor and director of the Marriage and Family Therapy Program at the University of Minnesota, has studied the effects of marital counseling and written about it for years. Although a licensed marriage and family therapist and a strong advocate of marriage counseling, Doherty cautions couples to be wary of certain types of counselors who may be more prone to undermine marital commitment than help the couple work through their problems.[1]

He points to two types of counselors who can lead couples astray—incompetent marriage counselors and therapists who have a hyper-individualistic approach to marriage.

"The biggest problem," he says, "is that most therapists are not trained to work with couples, and they see working with couples as an extension of individual psychotherapy. It is not."[2]

Marriage Counseling versus Individual Counseling

What is the difference? In an extensive telephone interview with Robert S. Paul, licensed professional counselor and vice president of the Focus Marriage Institute at Focus on the Family, Paul provided me with important insight. The primary difference, he said, is focusing on "who really is the client." In marriage counseling, "there really are three clients—the husband, the wife, and the relationship. They are all important, and you've got to balance that and figure out how to create an effective way to minister to three different clients at the same time."

In *The Divorce Remedy*, marriage therapist Michele Weiner-Davis further explains, "Individual therapists usually help people identify and process feelings. They assist them in achieving personal goals. 'How do you feel about that,' is their mantra. Couples therapists, on the other hand, need to be skilled in helping people overcome the differences that naturally occur when two people live under the same roof."[3]

When quarrels erupt in the counseling session, therapists who are not trained to handle the discord may feel overwhelmed by it and may, at this point, try to turn marital therapy into individual therapy. "This work is not easy," explains Doherty. "The problem isn't just that some therapists can't handle it. The problem is they don't know they can't handle it, and they assume that there is a lot of individual pathology going on."[4]

Paul takes this a step further. "Oftentimes because of counselors not understanding the dynamics, they get to a point where they themselves feel ineffective. Because the clients don't seem to be making progress—rather than admit they just don't know what to do to help them—they figure that if they can't help, it may be because the situation is hopeless." Some counselors, at this point, because of their own lack of experience and training, recommend divorce.

What should a couple look for in a marriage therapist, and what questions should they ask?

Weiner-Davis urges couples to make sure their therapist "has received specific training and is experienced in marital therapy."[5]

"The counselor needs to understand that the heart of what they need to do in a marriage counseling situation is to treat the relationship,"

Paul says. He recommends finding a marriage counselor who at least understands systems theory, the foundation of marriage, and family therapy. Systems theory sees the relationship as a system where one person changing affects the whole system.

In addition to training and experience, Paul suggests also asking what kind of approach a counselor takes: "Let them describe how they intend to proceed to see whether it feels like a good fit."

Weiner-Davis contends that people should "make sure the counselor is biased in the direction of helping you find solutions to your marital problems, rather them helping you leave your marriage when things get rocky."[6]

According to Doherty, "A recent survey of clinical members of the American Association for Marriage and Family Therapy found that nearly two-thirds said that they are neutral on the subject of marriage and divorce." In addition, he says, "If someone raises a concern about the fate of their children, many of us were trained to say that kids will do fine if their parents do what they need to do for themselves. That's what I used to say at the beginning of my career."

Even Christian counselors sometimes foster an individualistic approach and focus on self-interest, which pushes aside moral commitment as an important part of the equation. Questions that focus on whether spouses would be happier by staying or leaving the marriage reinforces the self-oriented spouse and undermines the sense of commitment at the heart of the relationship. This approach can unintentionally lead to divorce.

Asking a potential therapist questions like, *How important is it to you to help keep a marriage together and find solutions to the problems?* and *Do you ever recommend divorce?* can give spouses valuable insight. They need to know whether the kind of counseling they receive from that counselor will be focused on the hard work of wading through difficult issues to find true solutions that can save the marriage. Spouses who want to go to counseling may also ask the counselor, *What kind of results have you had in marriage counseling? How much success have you had?* Note what a counselor deems success. "If someone says, '100 percent stay together,' I would be concerned," Doherty says, "and if they say that staying together is not a measure of success for them, I would also be concerned."

Red Flags

A good marriage counselor can be invaluable in saving a marriage from the ravages of brokenness and divorce. But a counselor who is not trained in marriage counseling or has an agenda that is not consistent with the spouses' values can undermine or even sabotage their efforts at restoring wholeness to the relationship. Also, Robert Paul advises a potential counseling client to steer clear of a therapist who wants to give too much direction by telling clients what to do or counselors who start off with their own agenda.

If you are already in counseling and begin to feel uncomfortable, what are some red flags that this may not be the right therapist for you?

Taking Sides

"If your therapist sides with you or your spouse, that's not good. No one should feel ganged up on," says Weiner-Davis. "You should feel comfortable and respected by your therapist. You should feel that s/he understands your perspective and feelings."[7]

Taking sides can be as obvious as Janine's experience, quoted at the beginning of this chapter. Or bias can take place, says Doherty, when the counselor heavily concentrates on only one partner's problems and contributions. For example, if the wife is the only one to admit she has issues, the psychotherapist and the husband might decide the problem with the marriage is her mental or emotional state. The counselor may focus on her instead of both partners and the dynamics of the relationship.

On the other hand, Doherty adds that for a counselor who mainly does individual psychotherapy, the husband might be perceived as the problem if he comes to therapy to save the marriage but is not interested in delving into his own deeper issues.[8] In this situation, his unwillingness to endure individual psychotherapy might lead to a breakdown in the counseling relationship, and the husband may decide there is nothing to be gained from continuing. This is a situation where solution-oriented therapy might get better results.

Paul cautions clients not to immediately jump to conclusions, however, if they feel they are being singled out in a counseling session. Instead, evaluate whether the counselor is focusing upon one individual for the sake of the other person or trying to help one spouse for his or her own benefit.

Pathologizing Labels

Individual therapists who diagnose partners or marriages with labels that lead to hopelessness are a particularly insidious danger to restoring health to a marriage. An example given by Doherty is the person who goes to individual therapy, criticizes her spouse, and as a result the therapist "comes up with a diagnosis for the spouse, like 'I'm afraid you're married to a narcissistic personality disorder.' When you get a therapist giving you labels to pathologize your partner, it leads to hopelessness."[9]

Provocative Questions

An unfortunate way some counselors undermine or even sabotage a marriage is by using provocative questions that almost insinuate that a person is an idiot to stay in the marriage. Comments such as, "If you are not happy, why do you stay?" Or, "I can't believe you're still married to him" are inappropriate. Doherty says, "You'd be amazed at how many therapists say this kind of thing after a session or two. Without knowing it, what they are often saying is not that the couple are fundamentally incompatible but rather that 'I am fundamentally unable to help you.' Of course, this plays into the agenda of the distancing spouse who is considering divorce."[10]

"One of the things that is most distressing to me," Paul says, "is when marriage counselors are in a situation that appears difficult—and maybe on the surface looks untenable—they may tell the clients they ought to just get a divorce. Their situation is hopeless."

Counseling for Those Who Are Separated

If you are separated, you might have a spouse who is unwilling to go to counseling. Or if your spouse does come, your spouse may already have one foot out the door. How is counseling different for spouses who are both seeking reconciliation versus those where only one wants to save the marriage?

In our telephone interview, Robert Paul called this a "mixed agenda counseling situation." He stresses that spouses have no control over the other spouse who may be leaning out and wants an excuse to get away, but they can focus on who God is calling them to be in this particular set of circumstances.

In a mixed agenda situation, Paul said in his own counseling he works with the person who is motivated because "as the motivated one focuses on who God created him to be, learns to care well for himself and to love well—even if their spouse wants out—it increases the odds that there might be a positive outcome."

Realize, if you have gone to counseling alone to talk about your marriage, it is difficult for a therapist to assess accurately what is happening in the relationship with only one person's perspective. That is why the most productive approach is to focus on what you can do from your side. Look at your own issues and your potential for growth as an individual and a child of God. Be wary of therapists who try to diagnose a person they have never met.

MARRIAGE INTENSIVES

A marriage intensive usually involves either a weekend or several days of intense counseling with a small group of couples. Intensives can be extremely effective in helping couples identify and resolve issues that are eating away at their marriage. Paul, who regularly conducts intensives through Focus on the Family's Hope Restored, explained to me that because a couple can stick with their issues for days, they may be able to get to the core of what is really happening. Tremendous improvement may be made in a very short time.

One of the disadvantages of normal counseling, Paul says, is that in a fifty-minute session once a week, it's difficult to deal significantly with the three-pronged dynamic of husband, wife, and relationship. In most cases, after warming up for the first ten minutes of a session, they may have only a few minutes to work on the issues before it is time to wind down so both partners are able to function when they leave. Then, in the time between sessions, more issues often surface so at the next meeting meaningful progress may be hard to reach.

"A number of our clients who've had a lot of therapy experience said it was like a year to a year and a half worth of therapy in four days because we were able to get deep and stay deep until we figured out what was going on," Paul says. "Then we could come up with an analysis: 'What can you do differently with what you now understand to make this better personally and relationally going forward?'"

Many good marriage intensives are available, but there are two I personally recommend. One is Focus on the Family's Hope Restored at http://hoperestored.com. For those who are recovering from adultery in the marriage, a Hope and Healing Weekend, led by Gary and Mona Shriver, authors of *Unfaithful,* would be an excellent choice. You can see more at http://hopeandhealing.us.

EILEEN AND WILLIAM'S STORY

Finding a good counselor can make a tremendous difference in traversing the uncharted territory of a marital breakdown to find wholeness again. Story after story of success has been shared by couples who have seen marriages restored.

Eileen and William had been married ten years when they first went to counseling. William's job required extensive traveling, and each time he returned home to his wife and kids, chaos erupted. Life worked when they were apart but not together. Eileen and William talked to their pastor, and he recommended they find a counselor. When they met with their first counselor, he got some of their background, looked at them and declared, "I'm not saying you won't get divorced."

Eileen just stared at him, shocked at his words. "We didn't come in here because we want to get divorced. We came in here because we don't want to get divorced," she said. The word *divorce* had never come up between them. Neither of them had considered it.

When they left, Eileen was discouraged. "I can't go back in," she said to William. They eventually found a therapist who helped them feel safe, listened to their stories, and even shared stories of his own. It was the first time Eileen ever acknowledged in words that her brother had sexually abused her as a child. Once her secret was out, the empathy showed by her counselor helped her escape from her feelings of victimhood and shame, hidden in her subconscious for years. He helped her find God's faithfulness, care, and healing.

William's childhood had been difficult as well. He had come from an abusive, alcoholic family. Consequently, when they married, two people with a lot of inner turmoil came together. Eileen and William had never talked honestly about the ghosts of their pasts, and when they shared their individual struggles in the counseling room, they felt relief. Seeing the reasons behind their discord helped them look at life honestly.

Because of deep wounds from their youth, healing took a long time. But hope was immediate. The counselor helped William know how to give Eileen the freedom to be honest and gave them books to read. Honesty between them was the beginning of hope. In reflecting back, Eileen says, "There's something about realizing this person is for me. Finally, it's unhidden. It's not a secret anymore. Everything else doesn't have to be perfect because he loves me and is for me."

Each of them had counseling for their individual woundedness. Eileen worked through her shame, and William came to understand how he coped with life because of his alcoholic family background. No longer each other's enemies, they could confront their problems as a team. Encouraged to look at themselves, they were able to talk honestly with each other. Sometimes it was hard, but understanding what was behind the conflict helped them work through rough patches.

Eileen joined a sexual abuse support group, and eventually she and William joined a couples group where they could interact with others. The leader and her husband were counselors, and Eileen and William not only began couples counseling with them, but a lifelong relationship as well. Through the openness of their counselors, they began to see some of their own negative patterns.

"They taught us when things got rough between us, how to gently invite relationship by making it safe. That's the word," Eileen says. "You *invite* relationship. So, in the midst of an argument, you stop and you go okay, I want to invite that person in safely. We learned how to invite each other into where we were. We could say, 'I can see this is very hard for you. I hurt you. I understand. I get it.' Not shaming. Not 'Why would you do that?' Or we might say, 'I see you're getting angry, and I know the anger is not all at me. I know you're dealing with something inside. Can we talk a little about what is going on inside?'"

Although their children are grown and married, William and Eileen still occasionally go back for counseling, sometimes together, sometimes separately. "Because we're still sinners," she says, "I still run into my shame sometimes. And he's a workaholic. So I'll go, 'whoa—you're gone. Hear me.' But I come out of it. So does he. There's been a lot of change. Although we struggle, we're good together, and I know God put us together."

Counseling as well as other mentoring relationships can serve as a wonderful buffer in marital turbulence and provide invaluable help for restoring marriages.

It is also good to remember there may be other victims in the home who need counseling as well. Children often suffer collateral damage from the collapse of their parents' marriages and may need to express their fears and anxieties to a third party. A counselor who specializes in helping children may help extend healing to them.

HEART WORK

1. How is it working out with the two people you selected for support in Heart Work chapter 1? Make sure you have at least one or two safe friends with whom you can talk. Call one of them this week.

2. Ask your church about good marriage programs in your church or community. Go to the links page on http://brokenheartonhold.com and select Marriage 911 and Retrouvaille to see if you have these programs in your area.

3. Write down three resources you can use to find a good marriage therapist, e.g., Focus on the Family, a pastor or lay counselor at church, someone you know who found positive help from a marriage counselor, etcetera.

4. Write down one thing you learned from Eileen and William's story.

Chapter 6

Protecting Your Child's Heart

My heart is breaking for my son. All I can say to him is we need to keep praying for Dad. I can't answer his questions about when and if he's coming back. Do you have any guidance or can you recommend any resources? There's very little guidance for helping a child cope with this kind of thing. — *Beverly*

———————

Sometimes when I recall that desperate time in my life that was shrouded in confusion and pain at the beginning of my husband's and my separation, I see two young faces in the shadows of my memory. As I look back now, I spot expressions of confusion and pain on their faces too. But my overwhelming distress at the time shut them out from my conscious awareness. They were hurting, and I was their mother. But I was too overwhelmed with my own raw emotions to reach out to help them or even to know how to shield them from the havoc swirling around our home. It is a sad memory for me, filled with regret.

If your spouse has left, and you have children in the home, your anguish may be similar. In the midst of turmoil in the home and your unhappiness, the children may be overlooked. While your own mind spins in upheaval, they may watch in lonely bewilderment, absorbing painful words and actions. Their anchor may be gone. They may feel their security slipping away, and they may not know where to turn or what to do.

This is one of those times when your own weak humanity may feel all too frail and fallible, and as a parent caught in a swamp of emotional pain, trying to hold yourself together may be about all you can muster. And yet, there may be someone else, young and vulnerable, watching and disoriented, depending on you to be strong.

So as you ask God to help you take on the role of warrior in this marriage battle, how do you help your children get through this time and what do you do to protect them? Because I know what an important issue this is, I want you to hear from a survivor. My oldest daughter traveled her own journey through the chaos of our family's three-year separation and is now a licensed mental health counselor. Having endured that difficult time in our family's history, she has collected unique perspectives that add to the wisdom she regularly brings to her counseling practice. Let me introduce you to my daughter, Julie Wolf.

JULIE'S STORY

I can still remember, sitting on my bed in my college dorm, my friend on the other end of the phone with compassion in his voice.

"Julie, I'm really sorry to hear about your mom and dad—"

"What . . . what are you talking about? What's going on with my mom and dad?"

With the words that followed, my world closed in. As a college student on my own for the first time ever, I was in a little rowboat in the middle of the sea. My one source of stability had been a large ship within rowing distance that I could easily get to whenever I needed it. When my parents separated, it felt like that ship was blown up and sinking to the bottom of the ocean. I was alone. There was no one I could turn to for security or stability. All the security I had ever known was no more.

As the weeks and months went by, I painfully realized my dad had seemingly, quietly removed himself from all of our lives. He left my mom in his wake, who, from my college girl point of view, was completely in ruins emotionally. He also left my sister and me, who were unsure of what was happening. With my sister doing her best to grasp our new reality and be as supportive as she could to our mom, I, being the oldest daughter, quickly took on the job of trying to make all things better for everyone, particularly my mom. I saw her pain, and with each day that passed, I became more upset at my dad, more sad for my mom, and more alone. I didn't know how to help her, and I didn't realize that wasn't my job.

Looking back, I see that both my parents were coping in the only ways they knew how at the time. They did not intend to cause pain. They were both just trying to keep their own heads above water. I deeply respect my parents for how they both ended up seeking God with all their hearts and then using their pain and their story to help encourage others from making their same mistakes. They have allowed God to bring beauty from their ashes.

In the years since they reconciled, I have also had the opportunity, as a licensed mental health counselor, to help many parents struggling with how to love their children well through this very difficult journey of separation and sometimes divorce. I hope to share with you some of the practical things I have learned.

Children whose parents are separated walk through a painful journey which will be part of their story God will use to grow and mature them. Although there are many do's and don'ts for parenting through a separation, there are no perfect formulas and no guarantees. Your children will have to choose for themselves how they will walk through that story. If you are separated and a parent, you can do a few things to encourage health and reduce harm to your children. I hope to provide both encouragement and practical help as you seek to do the best you can for your children while navigating your own painful and difficult path.

SELF-CARE

Self-care must be your top priority. You may think this sounds selfish, but if you cannot care for yourself, how can you possibly take care of another precious little soul who depends on you? Think of yourself as the captain of a ship on which your child depends. If the captain is not well, the whole ship is in trouble.

Eat healthy meals, not just snacks, and make proper sleep hygiene a priority. Exercise is an excellent way to burn off excess stress hormones that can linger in the brain and hinder quality sleep. Spend time soaking in God's presence. This means you are not performing in any way but rather just being with him. Your experience of God's presence is not dependent on your reading the right passage of Scripture, singing the right song, or praying the right prayer. Rather, put on some praise and worship music, get comfortable, and use your imagination to picture yourself literally in the presence of God. What is his posture toward you? What words is he speaking to you? Remember, he loves you even in the midst of your heartbreak.

MAINTAIN ROUTINE

You may feel as though your world has been turned upside down, but make an effort to keep your routines with your children as normal as possible. Try to eat meals together, keep up with bedtimes, chores, and other previously established household rules. Make an effort to keep your children engaged with their friends and extracurricular activities. This will not be feasible 100 percent of the time, but children going through turmoil thrive in consistency and normalcy. Routines also encourage them that regardless of the outcome related to your marriage, their lives will go on and they will be okay.

SPEAK TRUTH AND ENCOURAGEMENT

Your children need to be explicitly told the separation is not their fault. This is a fear many children have. They need to understand that even when they hear you and your spouse arguing about them, they are still not the cause of the separation. They need to know you and your spouse both still love them, and the separation does not change that.

It's also very important you give your children space to express their feelings about what's happening. Let them know it's okay to experience both positive and negative emotions. Recognize they might be angry with you or your spouse and give them permission and tools to express those feelings in a healthy and respectful manner.

SAFE PEOPLE

In walking through a separation, make sure your children know some safe people to whom they can talk and where they can process their feelings. Safe people should be those other than you or your spouse. Do not allow children to get stuck thinking they are part of some big, dysfunctional family secret they have to bear all alone. If a close friend or family member can't fill this role, consider taking them to a counselor who can offer your children a safe place to process while ensuring confidentiality.

NO SPOUSE BASHING

Speak respectfully of your spouse to your children so if you do reconcile, your partner can step back into the family and resume a parenting role. Resist the urge to talk negatively about your spouse to your children in any case. You will never benefit in the long run by intentionally making the other parent look bad. Disrespect between spouses can cause the children to experience confusion. Generally speaking, children love both their parents and identify to some degree with each. When you verbally put down their other parent, your children often feel put down as well.

Similarly, don't tell your children age-inappropriate details about your marriage problems. Such details might include information about an affair, substance abuse, or personal issues with your spouse. Let your children relate to their parent as a parent without burdening them with unhelpful information.

LET A CHILD BE A CHILD

Do not seek advice, counsel, or comfort from your children, even if they want to help. This is not their role. By focusing exclusively on their parents' emotional needs, some children may be prone to deny their own pain, which can lead to self-destructive behavior. Remember, even if they do not show it outwardly, your children are hurting too. Denying their own pain to manage yours can ultimately damage your own relationship with them as they take on the role of your caregiver. I have heard parents say to their child, "We are here to support each other." No, you and your child are not available for each other as partners with equal responsibility of care. Even though you are hurting, your role as a parent is to support your child. Your child is not here to support you.

Be intentional about seeking support for yourself from other adults. If you do not have a friend you can talk to, it is critical to seek out the support of a pastor or trained professional. You will be unable to be strong for your child if you do not have a safe adult you can talk to when you are feeling weak.

DO NOT INTERROGATE YOUR CHILD

Do not question your child about time spent with the other parent. Questions like, "So, what is Dad (or Mom) doing this weekend?" are off limits. You may really want to know, and your children may have a lot of information. However, interrogating your children may cause them to feel as if they have to choose sides or choose between their loyalty to you versus your spouse. In answering, they will likely feel they are betraying the other parent, especially if they see you getting upset. Children in this scenario often start lying to their parent or shut down in an attempt to protect you. They may withhold information in efforts to please you and help manage your emotions. Instead, let your children know you want to be a safe person for them to talk to about anything. Similarly, do not send messages through your child to your spouse, even though it may feel like a convenient way to communicate. Your child will bear the brunt of this action.

BE AWARE OF YOUR OWN TRIGGERS

Realize your separation is not only affecting you, but your children as well. They may respond to this pain by acting out, shutting down, becoming the perfect child, or trying to become your caretaker. Most children, during a separation, still long for their parents to be reunited and may respond emotionally to the separation with denial, anger, or depression. Because young children and teens do not have a mature filter, questions they ask or comments they make may at times knowingly or unknowingly trigger your pain, anger, or despair. Be patient with them. Keep in mind your interactions with your child surrounding this topic should be to support your child.

Finally, remember you will never be a perfect parent. This is okay, and this is why we all need Jesus. Your child will learn that from you during this time as well. Keep surrounding yourself with people who can help support you as you seek to support your children. Self-care is a top priority. You and your family will get through this and have a story on the other side that God will use for his glory. Do not lose heart, "Let us not become weary in doing good, for at the proper time we will reap a harvest if we do not give up" (Galatians 6:9).

PARENTS WHO DID IT RIGHT

After thinking about my daughter's advice above, you may find encouragement in the two stories that follow. These are living examples of parents who wisely handled the situations with their children.

Darlene's Story

Darlene experienced the pain of marital collapse, both as a child caught in the thick of her mother's two divorces, and later as a mother herself reeling beneath the weight of pain from her husband's unfaithfulness. What she learned from the first experience gave her wisdom to apply in the second.

During her mother's first divorce, Darlene was forced to become a grown-up seven-year-old who not only suffered her own pain but propped up her mother in the midst of hers. The emotional strain of hearing too much about her mother's abusive husband weighed heavily on Darlene and caused her to grow up and be strong in ways that were inappropriate for her age. Her mother, in spite of other failings, wisely sought out counseling for Darlene so she could process some of the confusion in a safe environment.

When problems developed in her mother's second marriage, Darlene, now in her teens, became the sounding board for both mother and stepfather. Her mother expected Darlene to be there for her, but Darlene had grown close to her stepfather as well and bounced back and forth between them emotionally as each confided in her, accusing one another of affairs and unrealistic expectations. At seventeen, Darlene was processing the adult emotions of her mother and stepfather as well as her own. When her parents divorced, she moved out and finished high school on her own with a job and an apartment she shared with a friend. Several years later, Darlene found herself in crisis once again. Disaster hit her seemingly happy twenty-year marriage without warning. On her way with her children to meet her husband for dinner, Darlene received a phone call informing her that her husband was having an affair. Overwhelmed with shock, she remembered the burden thrust on her by her mother's divorces. She did not want that for her two sons. She sent the boys into the restaurant to meet their dad while she finished up her conversation in private. Later that night, after an awkwardly silent family dinner, Darlene confronted her husband and found the accusations were true.

Wanting to shield her children from the kind of pain she had endured as a child, Darlene knew she had to find a healthy release for the incredible pain sweeping over her. She did not want to involve her children. Darlene contacted a counselor to give her a safe place for unraveling the deep feelings coursing through her. She also found a few safe friends in whom she could confide.

It was an agonizing, daily battle as Darlene fought against the ugly demon of adultery that had come against her family, many times fearing her marriage was at an end. But through it all, she learned to obey God and follow his leadings. After six months, her husband became convinced that despite the hurt he had caused her, Darlene could let him back into their relationship so their family could be fully restored.

Darlene successfully spared her boys from the trauma that had taken place by leaving room for their father to remain in their lives without taking a toll on their childish hearts. Today, she revels in the joy of a fully healed and healthy marriage and a family where her children can enjoy life without the stain of unwanted information and damaged emotions that might have bled into future relationships.

"If you're still in the middle of your crisis and realize you've probably told your children too much, stop," says Darlene. "Don't tell them anything else. Don't sugarcoat it. Get professional help that can guide the conversation. You might start by saying, 'You know this is kind of overwhelming. My bucket is overflowing, and I need to get somebody to help us.' Then seek out a good family counselor."

Grace's Story

When Grace's husband left her and their two growing boys, he said he wanted a divorce. Grace was devastated, but immediately she sought out Christian friends and pastors with whom she could talk. She looked to God for answers and direction.

While she read Christian books and sought help from a number of other Christian sources to make herself strong, Grace also hunkered down with her sons on the bed at night and answered their questions. She read uplifting Christian stories with them, listened to CDs together with them in the car, and spent time with them individually to find out how they were feeling—both emotionally and spiritually. When she saw them floundering, Grace encouraged them that with God's help, they would get through this time.

With a tasteful balance between openness and discretion, Grace kept her children in the loop of what was happening as the separation from their father continued. God was her focal point. In her bed late at night, she wept bitter tears, but during the day she gave honest encouragement to her sons. Attention to her boys did not waver. Although they could see her pain, they also saw her trusting God.

A few years later, one of her boys said to her, "Mom, I'm so proud of you. You were in a tough situation, and you overcame." Grace's testimony nurtured much-needed faith into her sons' minds and hearts, strengthening them for future trials in years to come.

PRAYING A HEDGE OF PROTECTION

Throughout this battle, pray a hedge of protection about your children on a daily basis. Ask God to protect them so the enemy cannot use this crisis to get a stronghold in their lives. Pray God will bring beauty from ashes.

Also, pray the promise of Romans 8:28 that "all things work together for good to those who love God, to those who are the called according to

His purpose" (NKJV). As my daughter Julie said, the bottom line is we all need Jesus. You can get all the advice and listen to all the stories, but only God can guide you on the path he has for you. As you let go and put it in the hands of Jesus, he will lead you one step at a time.

HEART WORK

1. Have lunch or dinner with a supportive friend who is a good listener.

2. Plan meals for the coming week, remembering to keep it healthy. Then go grocery shopping.

3. Let your child plan a special outing with a friend.

4. Let your child hear you say something positive about your spouse.

5. Plan to do something fun with your child this week.

6. Make a list of safe people to whom your children can relate and who might be willing to be a sounding board for them.

7. Arrange some one-on-one time with each of your children. According to your kid's particular awareness of the situation, ask how he or she is doing and pray with that child individually.

Chapter 7

Stepping into the Prayer Closet

Tell me why a God who hates divorce won't bring reconciliation to a marriage that I'm praying for. — *Yvette*

I'm really struggling with praying for my marriage. What's the point of praying for my marriage to be restored if God allows free will and won't intervene? — *Charlotte*

I don't want to divorce him, but I don't feel like things will ever change. I've prayed, but maybe I'm praying wrong. Maybe I haven't been patient enough. — *Tess*

One question I'm frequently asked by those who want to see their marriages reconciled is *How do I pray for my husband or wife?* Each reader phrases it in different ways, but in each query, I hear the desperation of a hurting soul searching for answers.

Usually, for the heartbroken spouses left behind, the prayers that repeatedly grip their hearts are "Lord, save my marriage," "Lord, please bring my wife home!" or "Please make my husband love me again." As they pray the desires of their hearts, these are the prayers that leap from their mouths to God. These are the desires that burn within their souls.

God wants us to do this. God wants to hear our hearts. God wants us to come to him and pour out our heartache. He hears us and he cares. During the first painful hours, days, and weeks, these are probably the only prayers we're even capable of praying.

Some of us have grown up thinking God only hears conventional church-like prayers with formal language and correct theology. But God is not some far-off deity who sits on his throne and only allows us into court when we are proper. God is a personal God who loves us unconditionally, who came to us as a man to share our burdens. He understands our pain, and he wants us to bring it to him so he can hold us close and wipe our tears with the breath of his Holy Spirit. He wants us to know "the peace that transcends all understanding" as we "present our requests" to him so he can "guard our hearts and our minds in Christ Jesus" (Philippians 4:6–7).

Allowing God to guard your heart is an important part of the journey you are traveling. Your heart has likely been in shock and needs a safe haven while you work through the details of the coming weeks and months. For God to do that, keep him close by continually going to him in prayer, remembering always that "the Lord is near" (Philippians 4:5).

PRAYING FOR GUIDANCE

After you've poured out your heart to God and told him the desires of your heart, what next?

You are on a journey with twists and turns and forks in the road that will often catch you unprepared. Life does not seem to be playing by the same rules anymore. What has worked in the past is probably not working now. The rules have not only changed, but you may find yourself playing a far different game than you played previously.

While you are surprised by this game change, God is not. He sees the beginning of the road and the end. He sees the whole landscape before you. As you pray, place your trust in God; seek his wisdom and direction. Let him guide you step-by-step, decision by decision.

Through much of our lives, we trust in our own instincts, our own ability to make decisions and plan our way accordingly. When looking for direction, we talk to friends, Google questions on the internet, read books, and analyze the situation by pouring over every angle and possibility again and again. But in the midst of this chaotic time, God is teaching us that in fighting this battle, we must trust him, as our Commander, to show the way.

My former pastor, Joel Hunter, once told a story of a man who got lost while on a trip across the country. He stopped at a gas station to see if he could buy a map of the region.

"We don't have a map," the owner said, "but I'll go with you and show you the way."

When we are going through a separation or have a fractured marriage, we want to know what is down the road. We want to know how to get from point A to point B. But God does not give a road map or a GPS. He gives us himself and promises to go with us.

As our companion, he does not necessarily forecast all the turns we are going to make, but right before we get to a fork, he says, "Turn right here," or "Go past that light and then you'll see a curve in the road," or "The street name changes up ahead but keep on going." We may not necessarily see that we are any closer to our destination, but we know God is with us one little turn after another. As we travel this strange and unpredictable road, if we want to hear his voice and know when to make these turns, we need to stay close to him and be alert.

One of the Scriptures I taped to my wall during my separation was Proverbs 3:5–6, which says to "trust in the LORD with all your heart and lean not on your own understanding; in all your ways submit to him, and he will make your paths straight." When you meditate on this verse and let the words soak into your mind, you will see that trust begins with surrender—putting everything in God's hands so you can hear his voice.

If you are ready to step out of the way and let God take over, your journey will take a more positive course toward personal, internal healing so you can find the pathway to discerning God's direction. Many times, God speaks to you through his Word, "for the word of God *is* living and powerful, and sharper than any two-edged sword, piercing even to the division of soul and spirit, and of joints and marrow, and is a discerner of the thoughts and intents of the heart" (Hebrews 4:12 NKJV). When you read a passage that particularly captures your attention, chances are the Lord is speaking to you. In Psalms 119:105, David, who overcame numerous dangers and challenges, declares, "Your word *is* a lamp to my feet And a light to my path" (NKJV). God uses the love letter he wrote in the Bible to speak to us intimately and give us direction.

Sometimes God uses other Christians to give guidance, either through individuals, pastors, teachers, counselors, or books. Prayerfully considering what others say while always looking for confirmation through Scripture can be another source of direction.

At special moments, God gives us a nudge, a glimpse of truth, or a leading through quiet whispers in our hearts. As we spend more time with him, we will begin to discern his voice from the clamor of noise that bombards our ears and thoughts and gets in the way of hearing from him.

In *A Praying Life*, author Paul E. Miller confesses, "The great struggle of my life is not trying to discern God's will; it is trying to discern and then disown my own. Once I see that, then prayer flows. I have to be praying because I'm no longer in charge."[1]

Once we know we are no longer in charge, we will hopefully be ready to listen.

PRAYING FOR PERSONAL INSIGHT

If you are listening—seriously listening to what God wants to say to you—one of the first things the loving Father might want to talk about is you. Listening begins with an attitude of humility, praying in complete surrender to God, throwing off defensiveness to allow God "to know my heart; to test me and know my thoughts. See if there is any wicked way in me, and lead me in the way everlasting" (Psalm 139:23–24 NRSV).

As you walk through this dark valley, God wants to hold your hand and bring healing to those broken places in your life where you may feel rejection or abandonment, hurt or disappointment. He also wants to prune out the dead wood of sin. As you lean on God through prayer, he will show you the next step for your healing and then the next. And if you are walking with Jesus as your Savior, you can have the confidence that God will give you the good and perfect gifts he has stored up for you as his special child. Allowing God to minister intimately to you individually can be the key to seeing your most fervent prayers answered.

While the urgency of your prayers is probably focused on your spouse and the healing of your marriage, your life is not about your spouse. Your life is about you and God. Do not let your spouse become an idol you depend on as the source for your happiness and well-being. God will never forsake or leave you. Whether or not you and your mate become reconciled, God has a future for you. He has things to teach you as he walks with you through life. If your prayers are merely focused on your spouse and your marriage, you may miss hearing the personal messages he has for you.

Decide right now, at this moment, to put your spouse and the circumstances of your marriage on the back burner and focus on God. As you go to him in prayer, let him show you what he wants to do in your life.

IF ONLY MY SPOUSE WOULD . . .

In our marriage classes when we begin sharing in small groups, inevitably someone will say, "If my husband/wife would change and do the things he/she needs to do, our marriage would be okay." When marriages are in turmoil, the natural reaction is to cast blame on a spouse and sometimes others. Your partner's faults are so much easier to see than your own.

The Bible has an antidote for this.

> Why do you look at the speck of sawdust in your brother's eye and pay no attention to the plank in your own eye? How can you say to your brother, "Brother, let me take the speck out of your eye," when you yourself fail to see the plank in your own eye? . . . first take the plank out of your eye, and then you will see clearly to remove the speck from your brother's eye. (Luke 6:41–42)

After my husband and I were separated, it took me an entire year before I realized our problems were not all my husband's fault. Through a dramatic moment of self-discovery and humility, I saw how my own sin and shortcomings had contributed so bitterly to the problems in our marriage. By humbling myself under the sovereignty of God's cleansing hand and allowing him to sift me and show me the sin in my own heart, it became a turning point. As hard as it was to acknowledge my part in the collapse of our marriage, I also saw his fatherly love at work in his discipline and correction. He indeed loved me too much to leave me in my self-righteous state. He wanted to move me on to greater things. He wanted to purify my heart and let me discover the wonder of his grace. Not long after that time, I attended a Bible study on Hebrews. The text for that particular evening included Hebrews 12:6: "The Lord disciplines the one he loves, and he chastens everyone he accepts as his son." Having finally recognized the hidden offenses in my life, I had to say, "Yes, Lord. I accept your correction and ask your forgiveness for my sin."

As I came to him with a repentant heart, I knew my loving Father was wrapping me in his arms of grace. With his favor and forgiveness, my journey of faith moved forward into a new phase of the unknown, but beside me was the one who knew the way.

When we are seeking God's direction and healing, when we want his favor in answering our prayers, we must first ask him to cleanse our own hearts. Often, we are blind to our own shortcomings, but as we look into the mirror of God's Word, he will show us malignant spots in our character that need healing and hidden faults that may have contributed to the problems in our marriage. Even if your spouse's sin is far more egregious than your own, sin is still sin. First Timothy 5:24 reminds us that "the sins of some people are conspicuous, going before them to judgment, but the sins of others appear later" (ESV). Whether sins are more conspicuous or somewhat hidden, before receiving all God has, we must let him search our hearts and root out any wicked ways we have been unable to see, then ask his forgiveness.

As God convicts you of your own sin and you allow him to make changes in you, not only will you experience a renewed relationship with Christ, but a new dynamic may occur in your marriage. The changes in you can spur changes in your partner as well, and that may spin your marriage in a new direction.

ANN AND ROCKY'S STORY

Ann was caught completely by surprise when her husband, Rocky, told her he did not want to be married anymore. They had been separated twice before in the early days of their marriage, but the crazy days of their youth were past. Ann thought things were good now. Their son was sixteen, and she had been growing in her faith. But apparently her faith was the problem for Rocky. She was growing, but he was not.

"You're on a different level," he said. Then he expressed his opinion. "That's not how you feel," she would say. "I know you. That's not how you feel."

Rocky would look at their son Gary, and Gary would look at him, silently communicating their disbelief. "I just told her how I feel and she's saying I can't feel that way. Well, I do feel that way." Rocky saw her as overbearing—pressuring him to be something he was not.

That same afternoon, as they sat on the dock behind their house on the family ranch, Rocky told Ann he wanted to do his own thing. He was tired of all the responsibilities. He did not want to live this life anymore. He was over it. Later, she also discovered he was seeing somebody else.

Ann immediately went to her knees in prayer. Desperate to restore her marriage, she saw a Christian counselor, read the Bible, and pored over Christian books on marriage.

She felt the Holy Spirit telling her, "If your husband was off fighting in a war and he was taken captive, wouldn't you do everything you could to get him back? That's what has happened here. He's taken captive by the enemy. Pray for him."

In a Marriage 911 class, Ann's group leader shared her own testimony of realizing she had been self-righteous in her marriage. The words hit Ann hard.

"Oh, my, that's me! That's the way Rocky sees me. He says, 'You're further along in your walk.' But what he really sees is my self-righteous attitude." She wanted him to walk with Jesus like she did and understand the things of God. Now she realized that was the Holy Spirit's work, not hers.

Ann left Rocky alone and did not badger him. She did not argue, pressure him, or talk badly about him to others. She did not hound him about his faith. Ann had peace and knew God was at work. If the Lord laid something on her heart to say to Rocky, she said it, but she did not expect a response. She was going on with her life, and Rocky noticed.

One day Rocky asked to come over and talk. Believing this was going to be about divorce, Ann called her prayer warriors.

Sitting on the porch looking out at the lake, Rocky told her he thought they needed to move on with their lives. He never used the word divorce. Ann listened without arguing. She had a peace even when she realized what he was trying to say.

"If you want a divorce this is something you'll have to do on your own," she said, "because I know God does not want me to divorce you. It's not something I want to do, but I can't stop you."

Ann's response was not what Rocky expected. He saw a change. He saw her peace.

Years later, he said, "I saw a light in her. It was the light of Christ. Had she come after me and hassled me about things, we'd never be back together. We'd be divorced." That conversation was the catalyst that turned things around.

Rocky began going to church more often. During the following year, he moved from an apartment back into his sister's house next to their home on the family ranch, where Ann was living. Ann started a Bible study in her home and invited Rocky. He came often and usually lingered afterward for a while. Occasionally, he would stop by the house.

When they had been separated for two and a half years, Ann heard about Retrouvaille. She sent Rocky the information and asked him if he would like to go.

"If you're not interested in going," she said, "I've made the decision to move off the farm. I can't take the pain anymore of living here if you don't want to do anything."

Her words got his attention. Through Retrouvaille, they began communicating again. Gradually, they started dating.

Rocky would come by and say, "You want to go with me on a motorcycle ride?" "You want to get a bite to eat after church?"

The Holy Spirit was completely in control, and Ann was willing to follow his lead. Six months later, his sister had all of her floor tiles resurfaced inside the house, and Rocky had to leave the home. He asked Ann if he could come over and sleep in the guest room, and he ended up staying for six months. During that time, they gradually eased back into married life together. Several months later they renewed their vows during a weekend marriage seminar at their church.

Today, their lives are completely different. Each morning, Rocky makes coffee for Ann, and they pray together. Before they even get out of bed, each of them prays they will not miss whatever God has for them to do that day. Serving God is their number one priority.

Life is a journey of change and growth. This is a time for you to get alone with God and let him strengthen you. He can show you how to grow. As you come closer to God and put your trust completely in him, he can show you how to become more of the person he created you to be. But first and most importantly, go to him with a heart of surrender. Completely submit yourself to him.

GOD'S SILENCES

As we wade through the pain and confusion, there are times when we feel all alone. We pray but don't seem to receive an answer. Nothing changes outwardly.

When I read the story of Joseph in the Bible, I cannot help thinking he too must have felt alone at times while languishing in prison. Joseph had been righteous in all his ways. He had been faithful to God and resisted temptation. Yet, he was unjustly sent to prison for well over two years and forgotten. Was Joseph afraid God had forgotten him also? Unbeknownst to Joseph, God was preparing him for something bigger than he could have imagined. When the time was right, God released Joseph from prison and raised him up to be a ruler in Egypt. Joseph's imprisonment was not only about Joseph; it was part of a larger story that encompassed thousands of people in many lands.

When God seems silent and nothing seems to happen in answer to our prayers, we may simply be unaware of the larger story going on around us. While we look for immediate answers to specific needs, it might help to realize our dilemma is actually part of a bigger story. In the perspective of eternity, the events of our lives are not isolated, but woven together by the hand of God, each one affecting our own lives and the lives of others in ways known only to God. When God seems silent, we can be assured he is at work behind the scenes, weaving a story of eternal consequence in larger-than-life dimensions—ones we can't even imagine.

In his book *A Praying Life*, Miller talks about Joseph's story and sees God's silence not as a liability but an opportunity.

He explains, "When God seems silent and our prayers go unanswered, the overwhelming temptation is to leave the story—to walk out of the desert and attempt to create a normal life. But when we persist in a spiritual vacuum, when we hang in there during ambiguity, we get to know God. In fact, that is how intimacy grows in all close relationships."[2]

Despite our painful circumstances, or perhaps because of them, as we dig down deeper in prayer to find direction, we can become more sensitive to God's leading.

Prayer is not a formula, and it is not a means of manipulating God to get what we want. Prayer's greatest triumph comes from a deepening relationship and dependence on God. I often tell people that during my husband's and my separation, although it was the hardest season of my life, it also became the sweetest time in my relationship with God. I truly felt I was hanging in suspension, with God's hand holding me up above the quagmire that otherwise enveloped me. As a result of this closeness to God, I could often feel his leading in small ways—nudging me when to speak, when to stay silent, when to respond, when to hold back.

When we persevere in our trials, and our faith is tested under pressure, we begin to shrug off the worldly scabs that harden our souls and separate us from God, and that's when we can hear his voice more clearly.

As Miller says so beautifully,

To see the Storyteller we need to slow down our interior life and watch. We need to be imbedded in the Word to experience the Storyteller's mind and pick up the cadence of his voice. We need to be alert for the story, for the Storyteller's voice speaking into the details of our lives. The story God weaves . . . always involves bowing before his majesty with the pieces of our lives.[3]

WHAT WE REALLY NEED

As our hearts become enmeshed with his, we begin to recognize that what we really need to win this battle is not what we thought we needed at all. What we need is not a marriage restoration. It's not for your spouse to return. Not for your partner to fall in love with you again. The most important thing that will bring healing to a marriage is for both individuals—you and your spouse—to be fully connected to God.

If your spouse has strayed from God, if her heart is hard or if he has never known God's grace and forgiveness, God might be calling you to lay your spouse on his altar and pray for your partner's soul. God knows that oftentimes one must first come to a point of brokenness before turning to God for answers. Perhaps this is your spouse. Or perhaps it's even you.

God's first concern, even before happiness or a great marriage, is for each of you to be able to spend eternity with him. God disciplines those he loves because he wants to bring his children to salvation; he wants to purify hearts; he wants to be able to give you and your spouse the gifts he has in store for you, both on earth and in heaven.

While your heart's desire is for God to save your marriage, God first sees two individuals in need of him, two individuals he wants to shower with his love. As a result, God may be asking you to wait on him and take a giant step in faith by merging your prayers with God's highest calling for you and your spouse.

Because of the pain and loneliness, you may be tempted to take shortcuts and try it your own way, but it takes time for change to take place in each person so reconciliation will result in a brand-new, fully healed marriage. As much as you want your mate to come home, if he returns without having a heart relationship with God, chances are, he still won't be the partner in life you want, and your marriage would continue to be broken.

HOW THIS WORKED AND DIDN'T WORK FOR ME

During the early days of our separation, my husband and I went to a counselor who encouraged us to get back together and work things out from there. He followed her advice and did come home but then left again two months later.

What happened?

Essentially, nothing had occurred to make our marriage any less fractured than it was when my husband left the first time. Our situation was unchanged. God needed two and a half more years to make the necessary changes in each of us so we would experience a fulfilling marriage. I needed to lay my husband on the altar and trust God to do what was necessary to bring my husband back into relationship with God—whether or not our marriage would ever be restored as a result.

To merge your prayers with God's desire for both you and your mate, start with your decision to sacrificially pray for your spouse—not to come home or love you again, but for your spouse to discover God's grace—for your spouse to fall in love with God, for only then can God turn your spouse's heart back to you. Only then can the circle of love be made complete and a home become filled with the godly love that will give you the desires of your heart.

Praying for your spouse despite the pain she is causing you is not easy. In fact, it can feel like turning your heart inside out and giving it to the enemy to stomp on once again. Because I have been there and seen God's hand turn things around, I can now bring this message of hope to you. By humbling yourself before God in complete surrender, telling him you cannot do this, but want to, you will feel his holy arms embracing you and pulling you close. Within the safety of his loving arms, God's strength will infuse your weakness so you can dare to soften your heart and pray this sacrificial prayer for your mate.

Praying for your spouse to know God truly is the most powerful prayer you can pray to save your marriage and transform your life together. God can use all this for his purposes and for yours too. As hard as praying this prayer may be, God is taking you on a deeper journey. Go with him where he wants to take you. Go deep into his heart. Let go of all the expectations and desires you have for marriage and love and grasp onto that deeper love of God.

Restoration can take place, but no one can make that promise to you. As you walk with God through this time and trust him, let him unveil one truth after another for you so when you reach the other side, you will truly know God's heart. God wants a heart surrendered and devoted to him. If that is a picture of your heart, God will provide what you need and bring good from your pain. If you can trust God without knowing what the final outcome will look like, then you can walk this journey with him, pray for your spouse, and know God will bless you.

> I kneel before the Father, from whom every family in heaven and on earth derives its name. I pray that out of his glorious riches he may strengthen you with power through his Spirit in your inner being, so that Christ may dwell in your hearts through faith. And I pray that you, being rooted and established in love, may have power, together with all the Lord's holy people, to grasp how wide and long and high and deep is the love of Christ, and to know this love that surpasses knowledge—that you may be filled to the measure of all the fullness of God. (Ephesians 3:14–19)

HEART WORK

1. What are you leaning on the most to find direction for your marriage?

2. As you meditate on Proverbs 3:5–6, what do you feel God is telling you? Read "The Puzzle" in my book *Broken Heart on Hold* to help you meditate on this passage.

3. Have you had an epiphany moment when God has shown you the part you contributed to your marriage's breakdown? If so, write down what God has shown you.

4. Spend a day with God praying and listening for what God wants to say to you.

Chapter 8

Letting Go:
The Hardest Prescription

Right now, the one thing I don't know how to do is let go of my wife emotionally. I don't know what that means. Does that mean I stop loving her? Or to stop loving her as a wife, but just as a sister in Christ? Almost like accepting that it's over until if/when God says otherwise? I'm not sure I know how to do that. — *Ralph*

When it was her turn to share, Sheri opened her mouth to speak but quivering words caught in her throat. The woman sitting beside her in our small group reached over with a comforting touch, but Sheri bristled and shook her off. When Sheri tried to speak again, tears escaped behind her raspy words, exposing the pain she tried so desperately to hide.

"I can't talk. Let me just listen." For the rest of the evening, she sat quiet and stiff, body tensed, holding back the tears threatening to unmask her broken heart. During the following week her solemn, sweet young face lurked in my mind.

Having grown up in Christian families and followed the rules, Sheri and her husband were not supposed to be in this place of upheaval. But here she was with two small children and a husband who had left two years earlier to find greener pastures and more exciting rendezvous. Gritting her teeth and bottling in her surging emotions, Sheri had put on a happy mask and continued trying to be the good wife and mother she thought she was supposed to be. She was now at a breaking point, but still she refused to release control. Even in that safe place, surrounded by loving women, she was afraid to let go and surrender it all to God.

But what do I mean by letting go? How do you do it? When do you know it is time? And why is it important?

In my marriage ministry, I probably talk about letting go more than any other principle. It is also the one principle about which I get the most questions. Most people are familiar with the song "Let It Go" from *Frozen*, where Elsa stands on the peak of an icy cliff, spreading her arms to the wind and singing about letting go of the secret heartache that has held her captive as queen. That may be the first image that comes to mind when I speak of letting go.

But the letting go I'm talking about refers more to letting go of your need for control over the outcome of your marital impasse, and surrendering everything—your marriage, your heart, your emotions, your mate, and your life—to God so he can bring healing. This does not mean giving up on your marriage. It means completely letting go of control over your situation and trusting God for the results so he can do whatever he needs to do in your life and the life of your spouse. It means grasping hold of the truth of Romans 8:28, that "all things work together for good to those who love God, to those who are the called according to *His* purpose." (NKJV). Letting go means really believing this truth and completely giving the control over to God.

The reality is, when fighting for your marriage in the middle of a separation, letting go is the most important thing you can do to find victory. But it is also the hardest.

Our natural inclination is to hold on and try to keep control. We try to find answers on our own—perhaps by reasoning with the one who has left to show where he is going wrong. We read the books, listen to those who are wiser, and attempt to follow their advice. We do whatever we can to make things turn out the way we want, whether it is through confrontation, capitulation, or manipulation.

But for you right now, regardless of what you have done, separation is still a reality in your life. Your marriage is still in crisis, and your spouse continues to push you away. You probably are either falling apart emotionally, completely exhausted, or both. Maybe you finally realize you do not have the answers.

If this is where you are, perhaps you are ready to let go of control. For there is one who does have all the answers. God knows exactly what is happening. He knows what is in your heart and in your spouse's. He knows the hurts and fears that prevent you and your spouse from moving toward each other. God knows exactly what needs to change for the two of you to have a fulfilling and happy marriage, and he knows the steps to bring that about. He sees the big picture.

You can begin to release control by examining your heart to see if you are hanging onto your spouse so tightly you have actually made him into your god. You may be afraid that if you stop worrying, you will lose every chance of saving your marriage. You may fear that putting your marriage in God's hands will open the possibility that God may do something you do not like. Your fears and worries hold you to your mate. That small thread of worry, however futile, deceives you into believing you have a shred of control. However, the opposite is true. By hanging on, you give your spouse control over your heart and emotions.

On the other hand, if you put your husband or wife on the altar and give your heart to the God who holds the answers, he can guide you through the chaos and give you peace and joy.

Your spouse is not god. God is God. Your mate is not your life. He or she is only a fallen human being and cannot fulfill all of your needs. Your life is about God and what he wants to do in your life. Only when you let go of your spouse and put your focus on the Lord God Almighty will you be able to move forward and find the good things he has for you. Letting go means surrendering everything to God, the one who intimately knows both of you so he can work in each of your lives to bring healing and give you joy.

Jesus said he came to heal the brokenhearted and preach deliverance to the captives. That is what he wants to do for you, but you have to let him. You have to release the reins of control and give them to him so he can heal your broken heart and set you free.

THE PRAYER OF RELINQUISHMENT

In her book *Beyond Ourselves*, Catherine Marshall calls this giving up of control the "Prayer of Relinquishment."[1] It is coming to the full realization that God's ways are not your ways and his thoughts are higher than yours. If you are praying for God to work in your marriage, you may be praying for something good, something that seems to be in line with what God would desire. Surely God wants marriages to be restored. You know he hates divorce. But God may have something better for you that you cannot even imagine. Perhaps what you are going through is part of a bigger plan. When you trust God enough to put it all in his hands, that is when you let go.

But how do you do it? That is the question that comes up again and again. The question comes in a variety of forms: *How do I let go and still love my wife or husband? How do I let go and at the same time continue to believe for my marriage? How do I let go without giving up on my marriage?* In your fears and confusion, you may be thinking something like this: "I'm afraid that if I let go, I'll stop trying to win my husband back" or "If I'm still praying for my wife, it seems like that isn't letting go."

Letting go is not the same thing as giving up. You can let go of the marriage without giving up on the marriage.

Letting go means saying to God, "You know how much I want to be reconciled with my partner. But, Lord, you are the most important thing in my life. My relationship with you is even more important than my relationship with my spouse. I trust you to do what you want to do in each of our lives. Consequently, I give my spouse over to you. Do with each of us whatever you want. If you want us to be reconciled, then I know it will happen, but life is not about my spouse or even my marriage. Life is about you. Even if my spouse is no longer in my life, I will still have you, and you are enough."

Do not be afraid to cry. If you are in the process of relinquishing control, do not think you have to be brave and hold your emotions all within yourself. Sitting in your grief and allowing the tears to flow can be an important part of your healing. Jesus came to heal the brokenhearted. Release that brokenness into his loving care. When you let go, you are giving your heart to God so he can keep it safely in his care instead of putting it in the risky custody of your spouse or closing it up in your own unyielding protection where it can grow hard and cold. God will take care of your heart as he journeys with you through this difficult time.

During the three years my husband and I were separated, I prayed for my marriage to be reconciled, but for most of that time, I did not see that prayer answered. Indeed, God had something better in mind. When we did get back together, we had each changed so that we had a better marriage. Amazingly, God had even greater plans for us. It was from that painful experience that I wrote my first book, *Broken Heart on Hold*, and now this one, enabling me to minister to other couples in troubled marriages.

John 15:7 says, "If you abide in Me and My words abide with you, you will ask what you desire, and it shall be done for you" (NKJV). When we let go, when we focus on God, then we can abide with him. When God's words come alive in our hearts, then our will and his connect so closely that we will begin to see all the good things God has in store for us.

A TRUE STORY

When Yvette first contacted me, she was desperate. She knew her anger and resentment were pushing her husband further away, but she didn't know what to do. Her faith was shattered.

When her husband left, said he did not want her anymore, and talked about divorce, Yvette felt "defeated, betrayed, and left for dead." It seemed as if someone else was living in her husband's body. Everything he did was out of character. Because she could not concentrate, she lost her job and was overwhelmed with feelings of loneliness.

Desperate to quell the conflicting emotions that raged within her, Yvette turned to God for help. As she spent time in prayer, asking God to bless her husband and her marriage, she realized the first thing she needed from God was healing from her own fears and deep feelings of rejection from childhood.

Eventually, the relationship began to soften between Yvette and her husband. Seven months after I received that first email from her, Yvette wrote this message to me:

> Hi Linda. I held on to your book, *Broken Heart on Hold*. I downloaded it on my iPad and my iPhone. I carried it with me everywhere because each moment during that time was full of hurt. I kept it in bed with me for those nights I would wake up in tears, or to read before I went to sleep. After several weeks, it began to keep me from crying. The chapter about letting go is what started my journey to inner healing. I gave my husband and my separation to God, and I focused on ME.
>
> The amazing happened during my separation; after I let go, God showed me things I had hidden and never dealt with. When all my issues surfaced, and I faced them all and began to ask God to help ME, it made me see my husband through God's eyes. I understood him better and what was going on; I began to see past my pain to understand why he left and see what he was going through.
>
> Initially, all I could see was what I was feeling. So I left him alone and prayed. I began to focus on healing Yvette and left my husband and his healing to him and God.
>
> I think when I left him alone; and there was no arguing or me flooding him with why, why, why, it calmed things down and that helped us both.
>
> Weeks would go by and I would not call him. Then, he started calling me. Then he started asking me out on dates. Then he invited me to his apartment.
>
> He began to let me back into his life and into areas that had become secret from me. Then one night at dinner, he told me he did not want a divorce, but that he wanted our marriage. Simply put, I learned to trust God with my separation.

Yvette and her husband did get back together. When we had contact two years later, she told me, "Our marriage has taken on a new identity. God is so amazing and is answering prayers I prayed sooooo long ago."

OVERCOMING THE FLESHLY PULL

But even when you read this testimony and understand the principle, you may still find it hard to let go. The flesh wants to keep control. Romans 8:6 says, "For the mind set on the flesh is death, but the mind set on the Spirit is life and peace" (NASB). The natural inclination is to hold on, to try to be in control, to do whatever possible to make things turn out the way you want. "Letting go" is the opposite of what you are inclined to do. It takes spiritual muscle developed by looking to God on a continual, day-to-day basis and focusing on him while taking your focus off your mate and off your circumstances. Setting your mind on the Spirit by letting go will free you from the raging emotions and conflicted thoughts that hold you captive. If you are struggling with letting go, what can help you overcome the fleshly pull? How do you give those control reins over to God?

What you focus on expands. Allowing your thoughts to wander to your spouse affects your feelings. Consequently, in letting go it is important to surrender both your thoughts and emotions to God along with your will and desires. Since whatever you are feeling usually springs from your thoughts, focusing your thoughts on God instead of thinking about your partner can move you to a more positive place.

When you start thinking, *But what if she does this? Or maybe if I do that, he'll* . . . (fill in the blank), you may be wresting the control reins from God once again and trying to figure it out yourself. Whenever you start thinking about your spouse, pray for him instead. Surrender your mate to God once again. Then move on to something else.

If you have trouble keeping your thoughts focused on God and off your spouse, be intentional about your surroundings and how you occupy your mind.

Here are a few practical ways to let go:

- Listen to praise music. Pour your heart into the praise songs. Sing along with the words to involve more of your mind and keep your heart pure.

- Spend more time at church. Some of my most profound and meaningful experiences of "letting go" happened during praise and worship services at my church. When the congregation sang, "You're all I want; you're all I ever needed," the words captured my heart, and I fully realized their truth. God was all I needed. I meant it. And I truly let go.

- Listen to Bible teachers to feed your mind and heart with godly wisdom.

- Read Christian books to enlarge your perspective and keep hope alive.

- Read the Bible and meditate on Scripture passages. Put Scriptures around on your walls, mirror, and refrigerator so God can keep your mind on him. Find a Scripture that speaks to your heart and repeat it over and over to yourself whenever you are tempted to become obsessed with thinking about your spouse. When you are truly in pain, immersing your heart and mind in the Word of God and praying at gut level sometimes feeds your heart more naturally so you can go deeper to find that wonderful "peace beyond understanding" that truly satisfies.

- Begin journaling your thoughts and feelings. During my husband's and my separation (and other difficult times when my emotions have been in a whirl), writing down my thoughts and feelings and seeing them on paper freed me from the burden of carrying them around. Pouring out my heart made me feel better and gave me relief. The problem had not changed, but I was at peace. Whenever I write these thoughts and feelings in the form of a prayer, it becomes a concentrated time with God.

Journaling your prayers or feelings allows you to see your words on paper, and when you reread them, you may feel affirmed by their honesty and think, *Yeah, that's how I really feel. That's what I really think.* The words are no longer thoughts swirling around in your head. Your feelings have crystallized on paper. Not only may you feel better, but later you may see how your feelings change from day to day, or week to week.

You might even go back months or a year later and say, "Wow! I really see some changes in myself." When you write these down as a prayer, you are lifting them up to God.

- You can also redirect your thoughts by helping someone else going through rough times. Focusing on the needs of others prevents your mind from dwelling on your spouse and circumstances and interrupts those feelings that lead into an undertow of despair.

THE POINT OF SURRENDER

One night at dinner with some women from my marriage class, Marcela brought up the subject of letting go and what a difference it had made for her in dealing with the problems in her marriage. The young woman sitting beside me knit her brow with a perplexed expression and frowned. "I get right to the point of being able to let go," she said, pinching her fingers together as though about to drop something. "And then . . . I just can't do it."

For some people, that final act of faith is so difficult. They want the freedom that's offered. But to reach out and grasp it, they have to let go of what's already in their hands. And they just can't do it. Even though it means the fleshly nature will reign instead of God's will, many people find it difficult to trust God enough to put their lives in his hands. The desire to be in control holds sway.

But God, who created each of us, who created our world, who is omnipotent and sees everything, understands what's happening. He has answers we do not have. He knows your spouse inside and out, and he knows you. God loves you and will take care of you. Put your spouse and circumstances on the back burner. Put your complete focus on God. He will lead you, teach you, and give you the strength you need for the journey.

Letting go isn't easy; it takes perseverance and a daily surrender to the God who is the Alpha and Omega and the First and the Last—who holds all things together in his almighty hands. As you surrender it all to him, hold onto the promise of Romans 8:28, being confident that "all things work together for good to those who love God, to those who are the called according to *His* purpose" (NKJV). Each morning, as you fasten your gaze on the Savior, let go once again and allow him to strengthen you for the day ahead.

After you have let go and entrusted everything into God's hands, God can take the crumbling ruins and build something new on the foundations of your life. A new freedom and joy will begin to unfold as God shows you the new you . . . the you he created you to be and the future he has for you.

HEART WORK

1. Have you given your spouse space? And have you communicated you are willing to give it? Are you available when your partner wants to talk?

2. Have you been able to let go of your emotions and allow yourself to cry? If not, give yourself the freedom to sit in your grief. Yes, ask God to come and sit with you as you feel the pain and hurt. Do not stuff it out of the way. Do not grit your teeth and try to hold it back. Release it, let the tears flow, and give them to God.

3. Go to the Scripture page on http://brokenheartonhold.com and pick out a few Scriptures to download. Then tape them up on your wall, mirror, refrigerator, beside your bed, or anyplace else where you will see them often so you can keep your focus on God.

4. Pick out some praise songs that speak to your heart.

5. Buy a journal from the store and begin today by writing out your feelings. Put a date on it so you remember when you wrote it, and plan to do the same tomorrow.

Chapter 9

Unwrapping the New You

J ust wanted to tell you . . . I'M TAKING MY TRIP TO GRACE-
LAND IN JULY! Finally! God's been doing some amazing things
inside of me. I am still standing for me and my husband, but I have let
go and it feels so good! — *Chrystal*

When fresh wounds from the pain of rejection and heartache sear the
soul, individuals who are separated find it hard to think of little else.
They are obsessed with their circumstances and thoughts of their spouse.
They want to recover what they've lost. They want a sense of normalcy.
Usually, the only way they see a chance for this to happen is for their
spouse to change.

What husbands and wives in this situation don't realize is to get the
results they want, they need to be open to change in themselves as well.
And that is where the process needs to start if healing is to take place and
the marriage has a chance to be restored.

Whenever Marv and I start a new class for those in broken marriages, one of the first things I tell those attending is that to have a healthy
marriage, they need to have two healthy individuals in the marriage. A
large number of people come to these classes, pointing their finger at
their partner, saying if only he or she would change, they would have

a good marriage. Surprisingly, by the time the class is over, most have a brand-new perspective and have begun to see themselves with new eyes. At the end of one of our classes, a woman emailed me to say,

> I can't believe how taking the Marriage 911 class has changed me. Right after the end of the class, the Lord clearly showed the heart of bitterness in me and freed me from fear of speaking up. I told [my husband] what was hurting me and our relationship, and I requested his respect. After I spoke, I felt so free. Joy came from deep within. I know it's from our loving God.

Although her husband's actions were causing her pain, instead of focusing on him and the changes he needed to make, this woman realized her need to begin speaking up and expressing her own needs. Asserting herself, instead of passively remaining in the background, gave her new confidence and freedom.

If you are separated or have a spouse pressing for divorce, you have undoubtedly been thrown into a whirlwind of pain and confusion and may feel you are traveling a dead-end road. But your journey offers a unique opportunity to become the person you really want to be, a you filled with a confidence, joy, and peace no one can strip away.

You are beautiful to God. He loves you and wants to give you his joy. He created you to be a unique individual, replete with a host of gifts, talents, and distinctive qualities. You are a rare jewel, and he wants to help you become all he created you to be. You have immense value. There is no one just like you, and no one who can fulfill the destiny God has planned for you.

FINDING JOY

The apostle James tells us in James 1:2–3 to "Consider it pure joy, my brothers and sisters, whenever you face trials of many kinds, because you know that the testing of your faith produces perseverance." What? How can James tell us to have joy when our spouse has rejected us and we're facing the possibility of divorce? How can he tell us to have joy in the midst of trials? We don't want trials. We want happiness.

James tells us to have joy because he understood where joy comes from. He understood what joy truly is and what it is not. James understood that when we have joy in our hearts, it transcends what is happening around us, even when we find ourselves in a troubling situation like a separation or divorce.

Often, when someone is having trouble in her marriage, she bases decisions on the belief God wants her to be happy. Happiness becomes the goal. But happiness can be fleeting and elusive. It's transitory and depends on circumstances being good. Searching for happiness can become a distraction from seeking the more satisfying joy we really want. Joy is not the same as happiness, but deeper and more fulfilling. Joy frees us from our circumstances and brings a deep sense of satisfaction.

Your joy doesn't come from your husband or wife. It doesn't come from your work or your children. Your joy comes from God. In the midst of these difficult times, God wants to give you his joy, but Satan wants to steal it by bogging your mind down in your circumstances. Nehemiah 8:10 says, "The joy of the LORD is your strength." God wants to make you strong so you are not dependent on your situation to bring happiness. He wants to give you a deeper revelation of himself and the gifts he has for you.

When you put all your concerns in Jesus's hands, he will be with you and fight for you. Then, as you continue to persevere with God during this time of testing, as you let go and give everything to him, you will discover his gift of joy.

Claim the freedom God wants to give you by relinquishing everything to God, acknowledging that he has all the answers and you do not. When you do that, you will find joy in your new freedom from the burden of figuring it all out. As you bask in God's love and realize he will take care of you, you begin to find joy in who you are, knowing you can trust God to lead you, teach you, and give you the strength you need for the journey.

BE GOOD TO YOURSELF

Because of the stress of your circumstances, chances are you have neglected the one person who can actually make a difference in your marriage—you. In the Marriage 911 class Marv and I lead, the very first lesson in the workbook talks about the need to nurture yourself. Joe and Michelle Williams, the authors of Marriage 911, say,

> One thing we notice in people whose marriages are in crisis is that they seem to have lost a sense of themselves as individuals. The stresses of marriage troubles and everyday demands have replaced the simple enjoyments in life. . . If you aren't taking responsibility to meet some of your own needs, you won't have sufficient energy, peace, and joy to meet the needs of others. You can't give what you don't have, and if you make your well-being primarily dependent on others you become powerless; you're well if they do what you want; you're not well if they don't.[1]

This was true of Chrystal, whom I quoted at the beginning of this chapter.

When Chrystal's husband first said he wanted to end the marriage and did not love her, she was devastated and desperate to do anything she could to win him back. As the months wore on and Chrystal tried to let go, she got a job and began to make changes in herself. After a while, she and her husband reconciled for a period of time, but without fresh tools to build a new relationship, they eventually divorced.

In the many emails she sent me, her struggle to let go was evident. She earnestly prayed for God to intervene in her marital breakup and show her what she needed to do, but she was trapped in an emotional roller coaster that kept her anxious about her husband's actions.

When I talked to Chrystal shortly afterward, she was distraught that after all the waiting and praying, her marriage had ended in divorce. As we talked, it became apparent that one of the hindrances to her really letting go was that she felt beholden to the needs of those in both her immediate as well as extended family.

"Chrystal," I said, "You need to nurture yourself and think about what you want to do. What is something you've always wanted to do, but have never done?"

"I don't know," she mused.

"Is there someplace you've always wanted to go?"

I heard her laugh on the other end of the line. "I've always wanted to go to Graceland where Elvis lived." She chuckled again.

I laughed too, but in her secret desire to visit an Elvis icon, I saw the opportunity for her to nurture herself and truly let go. "Then do it," I said. "Go to Graceland."

"But it's expensive," she responded. "And it's hard to get away from all my responsibilities. Anyway, I always thought if I went I'd go with my husband."

For the next few minutes, we talked about Graceland—the challenges of going and the way it could help her let go. Two years later when I received Chrystal's email telling me she was going to Graceland and feeling so good, I rejoiced that she was finally letting go and experiencing the joy of doing it.

Although visiting Elvis's mansion in Memphis may not be the highest spiritual venture in a person's life, for Chrystal, this trip was the expression of freedom she needed to embrace God's wonderful love for her.

When Marv and I are leading a Marriage 911 class, the first assignment in the workbook is for people to make a list of activities they enjoy doing alone that are not immoral, illegal, or expensive, and then start doing some of them. Here are some suggestions:

- Go to a scenic spot to watch the sunset.
- Join a gym or exercise class.
- Take a long bubble bath.
- Buy some attractive new clothes.
- Get a new hairstyle.
- Watch a funny movie and eat popcorn.
- Swing on the swings at a playground.
- Try a new sport or rediscover an old one.
- Go to lunch or breakfast with a friend.
- Sit on your patio, porch, or lawn and eat something yummy.
- Tinker in the garden.
- Read a good novel.
- Find a pretty park where you can take a walk and sit for a while.

Do something enjoyable you used to do that you have stopped doing. When you are able to enjoy yourself in spite of what is happening with your spouse, you will feel more refreshed and grow more confident. For some of you, it may be an important part of the process of letting go. You do not put your life on hold when you let go, even if you continue to have your heart on hold. Letting go and getting on with your life are not incompatible. Just be careful not to close your heart off to God and his possibilities. Let God take care of your heart and live your life fully.

So give yourself a break. With God by your side, do something pleasurable. Allow yourself to meet some of your own needs without depending on your spouse to bring you happiness.

TAKE CARE OF YOUR BODY

Recently I spoke with a mental health counselor who told me she was amazed to discover that when people start taking better care of their physical health, their emotional and mental health improve also. When all those things begin to heal, it also helps their relationships.

During a separation, if you become consumed with worry, it is tempting to neglect your body. Exercising and eating healthy may be the last things from your mind. It takes intentional work to do what does not feel natural. But during this difficult period of your life, doing what only feels natural may not produce the results you want. First Thessalonians 4:4 says, "Learn to appreciate and give dignity to your body, not abusing it" (MSG).

If you are stressed out from a separation, eat more fruits and vegetables rather than too many sweets and comfort foods. These may taste and feel good temporarily, but in the long run, junk food can cause you to become more despondent and rundown. Resist any temptation to escape through alcohol or drugs, and do not try to take the edge off your anxiety by smoking cigarettes. Engaging in addictive behaviors will complicate your crisis and eventually escalate your feelings of despair and misery.

When you feel stressed, exercise is one of the best remedies. Exercise is known to release chemicals called endorphins that reduce your perception of pain, trigger positive feelings of exhilaration, and raise self-esteem. Force yourself to take a walk, jog around the block, ride your bike through the neighborhood, work in the garden, swim, or do low-impact aerobics. Even doing housework or mowing the lawn will help your body and make you feel better about your circumstances as well.

If you suffer from depression, insomnia, or panic attacks, visit a doctor to get the help you need. Doctors can help you transition into a more balanced and peaceful time of your life while God is continuing to work in your marriage.

ALLOW GOD TO MAKE CHANGES

As you continue to focus on God and lift your heart to him, open your eyes to what he wants to show you about yourself. Life is about growth. Let the Scriptures speak to you. Listen carefully to Christian teaching. Take time to answer the questions at the end of each chapter in Heart Work. Read my Heart Talk blog at http://www.lindarooks.com, and read good Christian self-help books.

Let God show you the truth about your attitude and expectations, the way you handle conflict, and your interactions with family. Ask family members and others close to you about ways they think you should try to improve yourself. Then humbly listen to their responses without getting defensive. As you begin to see new things about yourself you need to work on, take the necessary steps to make changes and allow God to transform you into the you he created you to be.

A MORE CONFIDENT YOU

When you begin to make positive decisions to move forward in your life, you will not only become a happier, more content person, but you will begin to see better, more confident ways to relate to your spouse. And as you reject the feelings of being a victim, you will become more attractive and able to project a more upbeat attitude.

With this new confidence, when you have contact with your spouse, be positive, but don't hang on every word and don't overdo your enthusiasm. Don't seem too anxious to talk, respond to texts, or get together. In fact, after you've been together or talked on the phone for a while, make a move to leave or end the conversation before your spouse does.

Be less predictable and less available. When your husband calls, you needn't always pick up the phone or change your plans when he wants to see you. Ask God to show you when to say yes to your spouse and when to say no.

If you're normally inquisitive about what your spouse is doing, instead of asking questions about her day, tell her something interesting you've been involved in. Be upbeat. But if you've normally been self-absorbed, listen to what your wife wants to tell you and respond with gentleness.

As you stay tuned in to God with each step you take, you can sometimes say yes to your spouse, sometimes say no, while always saying yes to God. He wants your marriage to succeed. Most of all, however, God wants you and your spouse to come closer to him. Let the Lord show you ways he can make you into a fuller version of yourself. Let him help you put your insecurities behind you and grow your confidence so you can step out in faith to win back your spouse's heart. But do it God's way, not the world's way. With God leading you, you can avoid the trap of merely trying to please your mate out of codependent neediness. Never compromise who you are in God. Be wise as a serpent but harmless as a dove. Open your mind to his leading. Always seek God for direction. He's the Commander, and this is warfare.

ALBERTO'S STORY

Alberto and Rita were inseparable during the early days of their relationship. They traveled to Italy, Germany, around the United States, and loved to party. Eventually, however, Rita began to grow up and get serious about life. While she pursued a college degree and then a masters, Alberto continued going out with his friends and getting high. Although he functioned well in school and work, life was full of drugs and addiction.

Rita began distancing herself. One night after a heated argument, Alberto angrily moved in with a friend. A week or two later, Rita told him she was filing papers for divorce. She did not love him anymore and had lost respect for him. Her words sent Alberto reeling. All of a sudden, he realized this was serious, and he began having flashbacks about everything he had done and who he had become. Because he worked every day, went to school, and functioned well around the house, he hadn't thought the drugs mattered.

Suddenly, Alberto saw his addiction did matter. Something had to change. One afternoon, Alberto was deep in thought when he felt God whispering to him.

"It's time. It's time to give all this up. It's time to come to me." At that moment, God became real to Alberto.

He started crying. "God," he said, "I'm here. Just take it; take it all from me. I don't want this anymore. I'm giving it to you. That's what I want to do." A warmth came over him. That very week he found a new church and joined a men's group that began to help him. He never missed their weekly sessions.

Over the next few weeks, Rita began to see he had become gentler. He was not taking things personally. He even apologized. She asked him if he wanted to hang out and talk, not about them, but just to catch up. Rita appeared baffled when Alberto said he could not because of a meeting, a men's group.

"What's going on?" she asked. "What men's group?" When Alberto told her it was a group at church, it was not what she expected. A few nights later, they had dinner and talked about what they had been doing. Rita was curious about the changes. "Are you still smoking weed?"

"Actually, I'm not."

"You don't have a craving for it?"

"No." he said. "God's healing me up right now. I like where I'm at and what I'm doing. I want us back too, but I'm not going to push anything. I'm just going to let God take his course and do what he needs to do."

Rita was stunned at the change.

A week later, they went to church together and saw an announcement in the bulletin about an upcoming marriage class. During the class, they each spent a day with God, independently. That day, Alberto truly dedicated his life to Christ. When they started praying together, they felt the power of the Holy Spirit and began to put God in the center. Alberto was no longer anxious and worried. He felt comfortable and safe. God was in control.

Slowly, they moved back in together. He slept in the guest room at first. Meanwhile, they got involved in church. When they had their first argument, they realized things were truly different. Instead of lashing out at each other when their anger reached a peak, they each went to a separate room to get back in touch with God and pray, then came back, prayed, and cried.

Today Alberto is a different person—more confident and at peace.

He explained, "In the past I didn't want to be judged, but now I feel safe in expressing myself or taking a risk—either a career move, or with friendships, or opening up in a group." When Alberto allowed God to unwrap the new man within him, not only did he experience the personal satisfaction of who he had become, but he also reaped the benefits of a new marriage.

HEART WORK

1. Write down three positive qualities in yourself and thank God for making you into the unique person you are.

2. What are three things you will commit to doing this week to nurture yourself?

3. What exercise did you do this week? Write down a plan for the next three months as to what you will do to exercise your body. What else can you do to take care of your body in a healthy way?

4. Ask a family member or someone close to you about something you should try to improve in yourself, and humbly listen to what that person says without getting defensive. In the new journal you started after reading the "Letting Go" chapter, write down what that person said and what you think about it.

Chapter 10

Turning the Prayer Closet into Your War Room

I just came back from church and the pastor talked about going deeper. Perhaps that's what I need to do. Just hand everything over to God? And pray? — *Abby*

Now that you have considered your strategies, assembled support, and surrendered the reins to God, you are ready to turn the prayer closet into your war room. In this place of surrender, the powerful God of the universe empowers you to wage war in his name.

As you turn your attention to war and how to fight for your marriage, you must start by again recognizing the enemy who wants to destroy your marriage, and realize this enemy is not the spouse who left. It's the same enemy who not only wants to crush us but wants to undermine our God and all he has planned for us. Ephesians 6:12 says, "For our struggle is not against flesh and blood, but against the rulers, against the authorities, against the powers of this dark world and against the spiritual forces of evil in the heavenly realms."

We must understand the kind of battle we are facing and how to enter this new phase of prayer. How do we fight against an enemy we can't even see? An enemy who lies to us and is set on the destruction of marriages?

Our first act of spiritual warfare is to acknowledge the Mighty One who leads the battle, the Creator of the universe and the Lord of hosts who is the King of kings and the Judge of all the earth. If we want to win the battle, we must know our Commander and follow him. We must fix our eyes on him and the power he is able to give us. And we do this, according to Psalm 100:4, by entering "into His gates with thanksgiving, And into His courts with praise" (NKJV).

ENTERING HIS COURTS WITH PRAISE

Yes, as we follow God into battle, we come into his presence by entering his courts with praise.

If we truly want to enter into God's presence and hear his voice, if we want to pierce the darkness and shed the earthly scales that envelop our minds and hearts, if we want to experience his power, the path to this profound blessing of God is by entering through the gates of praise.

As earthly beings formed from dust, it is hard to transcend the physical world with all its enticing and demanding sights, sounds, and smells so we can connect with a God who often seems remote and unavailable to the physical senses. When we praise God, we remind ourselves of who he is: "For you, LORD are the Most High over all the earth; you are exalted far above all gods" (Psalm 97:9).

When words of praise form on our lips, we magnify God. And as he becomes larger, the enticements and demands of the world become smaller and less significant. That is when we can enter the presence of God.

In praise, we acknowledge the Lord is higher than the heavens—higher than our problems, fear, and Satan or any of his plans. We become stronger, not because we are personally stronger in and of ourselves, but because God is stronger within us. With his strength, God gives us courage to stand against the enemy.

Praise as a Weapon

Praise is one of the most powerful weapons we have in our arsenal. It not only brings healing to ourselves but it penetrates the darkness around us and begins the work of dismantling the enemy's plans. When Paul and Silas praised God in prison, the gates sprang open and their chains came loose (Acts 16:25–26). When King Jehoshaphat and his soldiers went to war by praising God, the mighty enemy armies that threatened them were defeated. "Our God, . . ." Jehoshaphat cried, "we have no power to face this vast army that is attacking us. We do not know what to do, but our eyes are on you" (2 Chronicles 20:12).

God's Word came to him. "'Do not be afraid or discouraged because of this vast army. For the battle is not yours, but God's'" (2 Chronicles 20:15).

In the morning, "Jehoshaphat appointed men to sing to the LORD and to praise him for the splendor of his holiness as they went out at the head of the army, saying: 'Give thanks to the Lord, for his love endures forever'" (2 Chronicles 20:21). And without lifting their weapons for battle, Jehoshaphat's army won the battle.

Can you imagine an army entering into battle by singing praises to God? That's what Jehoshaphat's army did, and the enemy was defeated.

God sometimes asks us to do something that, in ordinary circumstances, seems completely contrary to what the situation would require. Perhaps that's why Scripture calls it a "sacrifice" of praise.

A Sacrifice of Praise

As you approach God's throne with a hurting heart to fight for your marriage, you may be in so much pain that praising God is the last thing you feel like doing. You want to question God, to ask him why, to tell him what you want. You may even be mad at God.

But at times like this, if you can lift your voice in praise—even if it is just in an act of obedience, it becomes what Hebrews 13:15 calls a "sacrifice of praise" that is pleasing to God. Instead of giving into your fleshly emotions and your right to feel discouraged and forsaken, you offer words of praise to lift God high above the difficult circumstances that are bringing you down, to declare him the mighty King of the universe.

In Psalm 7:17, after recounting a list of grievances and asking for God's deliverance, David ends his petition to God by declaring, "I . . . will sing praise to the name of the LORD Most High" (NKJV). Time after time, when danger or suffering engulfed him, David poured his heart out to God, and he almost always ended his plaintive cries by lifting up the name of God in praise. Praise brings God near. David knew that. David experienced that. We can too. Once our sacrifice of praise truly gives us a heart of praise, true warfare against the enemy begins to take place.

Praise That Brings Healing

Praise can heal a heart's brokenness. During praise, the Holy Spirit brings to us a revelation of God's intimate, breathtaking love that pierces our hearts and breaks through spiritual strongholds.

Praise not only opens us up to more of God and his presence, but as we enter his gates, we experience his love more intimately. God is magnified in our hearts and minds. It is too amazing to even imagine as we begin to recognize that our Lord—who is the great I Am, the Alpha and Omega and the one who holds power in the palm of his hand—is also "the God who sees me" (Genesis 16:13). The realization that this mighty God who holds all things together is also our loving Father who wants to bless his children and give us the desires of our hearts is almost too much to fathom.

Time and again during my three-year separation from my husband, listening to praise songs held me together and gave me strength when depression and hopelessness threatened to pull me under. One day when I came home with an especially heavy heart, I felt the enemy dragging me lower and lower. I was desperate for something to cling to. I trudged into the house and went immediately to the music center with the intention of listening to my favorite praise music. But the music tape I wanted was not there. This was before CDs. My daughter watched me curiously as I ran from room to room, desperately looking for what I knew was the one thing that would give me peace. When I finally found it, inserted it into the player, and heard the music begin to soar through the house, my spirits lifted. Taking a deep breath, I began to relax and silently uttered my thanks to God for being my rock and strength.

In *Broken Heart on Hold,* I tell of another significant event during our separation when I found healing during an extended praise service.

At a time my husband and I were beginning to reconcile. . . my emotions continued to pull me in different directions . . . and as I worshipped and praised God from the depths of my heart, I felt the Holy Spirit washing through my emotions, churning through the memories, draining the anguish from my soul, cleansing away my pain to replace it with his peace.[1]

Praise as a Beacon of Light

Praising God shines light into the realm of darkness where Satan attempts to hide God's goodness. When we praise and worship God, our praise fills the atmosphere around us. Even in the home or car, praise music and Scripture songs can help us in warfare, causing the demonic world to tremble and scatter. God's Holy Spirit moves through the music and wars against whatever evil is present.

Light especially shines forth when our praises declare God's marvelous works by quoting promises from Scripture or personal blessings God has bestowed on our own lives. Remembering these and lifting them up to God glorifies him, builds up our faith, and brings us further into his light where darkness cannot dwell. Psalm 105:5 says, "Remember the wonders he has done, his miracles, and the judgments he pronounced."

Finally, praise can break through the silences. When you praise God, he is near. He is with you. He is in you. He inhabits our praises (Psalm 22:3), and you are more open to hear his voice. In the middle of praising God, you may hear God speaking to you in the still, quiet places of your heart as the Holy Spirit begins to break through the strongholds that have kept out the light. God may give you a word of encouragement, a word of direction, or a new clarity about your situation.

During a special morning of praise when I was listening to beautiful worship music and praying about a painful and perplexing situation, God opened my eyes to his larger purpose in the life of someone dear. He showed me the present pain would not be without reward both in this life and the next, and it would bring glory to his name and blessings to others. As I allowed God to take his sovereign place as King in my heart and emotions, God showed me how to pray for these circumstances and for those involved. Sorrow carved out a deeper place for praise and a deeper experience of God's love and presence.

The power of praise is a mystery, but for the children of God, it is a personal weapon that brings the powerful God of the universe to their rescue.

WRESTLING AGAINST THE ENEMY

With hearts humbled and open to God and with praises to him on our lips, it is time to devise a battle plan.

To wrestle against the enemy, all good soldiers need to learn how to protect themselves and devise a strategy that is more powerful than the enemy. For those who are separated and fighting for their marriages, they can begin by putting on the armor of God. Paul says,

> Finally, be strong in the Lord and in his mighty power. Put on the full armor of God, so that you can take your stand against the devil's schemes. For our struggle is not against flesh and blood, but against the rulers, against the authorities, against the powers of this dark world and against the spiritual forces of evil in the heavenly realms. Therefore put on the full armor of God, so that when the day of evil comes, you may be able to stand your ground, and after you have done everything, to stand. Stand firm then, with the belt of truth buckled around your waist, with the breastplate of righteousness in place, and with your feet fitted with the readiness that comes from the gospel of peace. In addition to all this, take up the shield of faith, with which you can extinguish all the flaming arrows of the evil one. Take the helmet of salvation and the sword of the Spirit, which is the word of God. And pray in the Spirit on all occasions with all kinds of prayers and requests. (Ephesians 6:10–18)

As you prepare to put on the armor, realize as you take your stand, you are not alone. Jesus is fighting for you, and he holds victory in his hand. This is the armor he gives you so you can clothe yourself with his truth and righteousness and be strong in his mighty power. With his armor securely fastened about you, you can face the enemy with confidence knowing "the Lord will fight for you, you need only to be calm" (Exodus 14:14 NLT). Remember, if we are believers and have put on Christ, the major battle of our lives is already won.

The first piece of armor is the belt of truth. Before we march into battle, we must wrap about ourselves the truth of Scripture, the Word of God, Jesus Christ, and him crucified. Without this foundation of truth, we are vulnerable to Satan's deception and seduction. A solid foundation of truth prevents us from compromising and shifting with any new wind of belief we may encounter as we enter into warfare. Paul also encourages, "Each one should build with care. For no one can lay any foundation other than the one already laid, which is Jesus Christ" (1 Corinthians 3:10–11). Allow God to purge you of wrong belief and purify your intentions by praying Psalm 139:23–24, "Search me, O God, and know my heart; test me and know my thoughts. See if there is any wicked way in me" (NRSV).

The next piece of armor is the breastplate of righteousness. We know we are not righteous. For Scripture says, "There is no one who is righteous, not even one" (Romans 3:10 NRSV). Righteousness comes from Jesus alone. He died on the cross so we could replace our garment of sin with his robe of righteousness. Only as a child of God can we have a breastplate of righteousness. And as we live out the righteousness Jesus has given us, we will crucify the sinful nature and begin to bear fruit— the fruit of the spirit.

"The fruit of the spirit is love, joy, peace, patience, kindness, goodness, faithfulness, gentleness, self-control; against such there is no law" (Galatians 5:22–23 RSV). As we begin to battle Satan's lies, we need to clothe ourselves with God's provision for walking in the character of the Holy Spirit by receiving these fruits of the spirit. If we exhibit the fruits of the spirit when conflict arises, we will react in the power of the Holy Spirit rather than relying on our own fleshly understanding and natural reactions. Our breastplate of righteousness, burnished with the glory of God, shines before us as we go into battle, blinding the enemy of his lies and confusing those who expect to see us responding in the flesh.

Feet fitted with the readiness that comes from the gospel of peace is the next part of our apparel. Are you ready to move forward when the Holy Spirit leads? If you have done the work in the prayer closet, you should be waiting with a humble spirit to speak words of life and peace when the Holy Spirit provides the opportunity.

The shield of faith, which extinguishes all the flaming arrows of the evil one, comes next. Second Corinthians 5:7, says, "for we walk by faith, not by sight" (RSV). What you see with your eyes can sometimes deceive you from trusting what God is doing behind the scenes. As you stay grounded in God's Word, you need to hold up the shield of faith when Satan comes against you so you can extinguish the lies he will continually shoot at you. Every circumstance you encounter offers the opportunity to believe God or to believe the lies of Satan. If you believe Satan's lies, they will cause you to wither up in confusion and doubt. But when you hold up that shield of faith, truth wins out and God moves you one more step toward victory.

As a child of God, the helmet of salvation is your ultimate protection in this battle. Before you can even contemplate going into battle against the evil one, you must make sure you are covered in the power of Jesus's blood, which comes when you accept his gift of salvation for the forgiveness of your sins. If you have not accepted Jesus as your Savior and Lord, do not even think about engaging in spiritual warfare. If this is a step you want to take, you can pray the prayer of salvation printed at the end of this chapter.

When you wear the helmet of salvation, you know who you are in Christ Jesus. You belong to him. He dwells within you. His blood has released you from the bondage of sin. His resurrection has given you new life. You are covered in his righteousness.

Next take the sword of the Spirit, which is the Word of God. Now that you are covered with God's protection, it is time to take up the weapon God has given you for battle. Speaking God's Word into your situation causes the enemy to tremble for he knows its power. "For the word of God is living and active, sharper than any two-edged sword, piercing to the division of soul and spirit, of joints and marrow, and discerning of the thoughts and intentions of the heart" (Hebrews 4:12 RSV).

Not only does the Word of God carry truth but it is also a weapon against the enemy. Spend time in the Word so God can reveal his truth to you and give you the powerful, life-giving words that will demolish the strongholds threatening your marriage. Find specific passages that apply to your situation and ask God to lead you in how to speak their truth into your circumstances. Then speak them boldly as you lift prayers and praise to God and begin to confront the enemy. God's promises are true. His Word is true. Use his words and promises to apply pressure against what is false and ungodly.

Once, I was praying for someone whose anger had become uncharacteristically abusive after having been enmeshed in a very negative environment over a period of time. I began to pray continually that she would "be made new in the attitude of [her] mind and to put on the new self, created to be like God in true righteousness and holiness" (Ephesians 4:23–24). Over and over, I used this Scripture and waged spiritual warfare, praying that this person would "be transformed by the renewing of [her] mind" (Romans 12:2). In months, she became a completely new person and was truly transformed by the renewing of her mind.

Bringing God's Word to bear on a situation has power to bring healing. Apply pressure continually against the enemy until he capitulates. Wrestle against satanic forces, not with them. For as 1 John 4:4 says, "the one who is in you is greater than the one who is in the world." God promises the victory when believers push against the enemy in Jesus's name by using the sword of the Spirit.

Finally, pray in the Spirit on all occasions. Be sure to keep in touch with your Commander so you do not miss his cue.

POWER TO CONFRONT THE ENEMY

Where does the power come from to fight against the enemy? The power comes from the name of Jesus and the blood of Jesus. Our authority comes from the power we can claim as sons and daughters of God and believers in Jesus who are redeemed by his death and resurrection.

Whenever we face the enemy, we must only do so with the authority we have in the name of Jesus and the power of his blood. We must only do this as believers who wear the helmet of salvation.

Throughout the Bible Jesus is given many names. Each of these names has power, and if you call on him by using one of these names you are also focusing on a particular aspect of his authority and bringing it to bear on your particular situation. Jesus is called the Lord of Hosts. As the Lord of Hosts, he brings his army of angels into battle. Psalm 24:8, 10 says, "Who *is* this King of glory? The LORD strong and mighty, the LORD mighty in battle. . . Who is this King of glory? The LORD of hosts, He *is* the King of glory" (NKJV). When you call on the Lord of Hosts, you are calling Jesus to lead his angels into battle on your behalf. For it is by Christ's power the battle will be won. He is fighting for you.

PRAYER OF SALVATION

If you want to wear the helmet of salvation and begin a journey of faith with God, please pray the following prayer:

> Dear Lord, I believe you gave your Son Jesus to die for me and my sins. I thank you for your love and forgiveness. Jesus, I accept you as my Savior and Lord and acknowledge the amazing sacrifice you made on the cross so I could have eternal life. I ask you to forgive me for my sins, and I give my life to you so you can make me into the person you want me to be. I want to live my life for you from this time forward. Amen.

HEART WORK

1. Put on praise music and sing along with it. Pick out some YouTube praise videos to watch. Play praise music in the car.

2. Commit to spend time in God's Word daily. Choose a book of the Bible or a Bible study guide and let God gird you with his belt of truth as you read the Bible on a regular basis.

3. Which fruit of the spirit do you have the most trouble exhibiting in your life? Ask God to strengthen this in you, and the next time you

see your spouse or experience conflict, make a point of letting that "fruit" control your response and reaction.

4. Look for specific passages of Scripture that apply to your situation. Then pray aloud, praising God and speaking your chosen Scripture in prayer over your marriage and/or your spouse.

5. Have you asked Jesus into your life to be your Savior and Lord? Have you confessed your sins to him and accepted his gift of salvation? If you have the slightest doubt, pray the prayer at the end of this chapter. Without Jesus as your Savior and Lord, the rest of this will have little effect.

Chapter 11
Making Tough Choices

His drinking has gotten to where I no longer want to deal with him or the marriage. He won't admit he's an alcoholic or even has a problem. I gave him an ultimatum and told him he had to choose the alcohol or our marriage. He said he was not going to stop drinking and if I didn't like it I could leave. I suggested counseling and he is refusing. I am just so tired of trying to fix him and our problems. I have asked him for a separation. Your help and guidance would really be appreciated. — *Maggie*

He continually tells me how much he loves me and doesn't want to be without me. He says he wants us to finish together. Unfortunately, however, he just can't get past the other woman. Five days after he came home he was texting her again. So I told him no more. He said, "I'm trying, what do you want me to do?" — *Barbara*

When fighting for your marriage during a separation, sometimes you need to take your gloves off and get down on your knees. Other times, however, you must put the gloves on so you can create safety for your home and children and protect your own heart. Finding that fine line between the two requires discernment, courage, determination, and tough love.

For some of you, it is simply a matter of continuing to remember the counsel of Proverbs 4:23 to "guard your heart, for everything you do flows from it."

Many spouses have to make tough decisions as they fight the vermin of addiction, adultery, anger, abuse, or other toxic behavior threatening to destroy their lives and families. A *heart guard* protects both the spouse who has been left and the spouse who is leaving. It also honestly and firmly reroutes the direction of the marriage so necessary changes are able to take place.

SEPARATION ISSUES

Before addressing the more serious issues of infidelity, addiction, and abuse I want to first answer some of the following questions that often arise regarding common issues of separation.

1. He's still out of the house but we text and occasionally speak on the phone. Lately, our communication is less, but he's made a few late-night visits home to "be with me," and I wanted to know your take on that. I have not been contacting him; I only respond when he contacts me now. Do you have any advice for me?

God wants us to love our husbands and wives even when they don't deserve it, just as God loves us when we don't deserve it. But expressing unconditional love still requires wisdom, and sometimes a "no" is prudent. Marriage is meant to include an intimate relationship with your spouse, but if your husband has left and cannot make a commitment to you or the marriage, then he has broken that intimacy. You need to let God guide you in what your relationship will look like until the marriage is restored.

You need to protect your heart. If your spouse is straddling both sides of the line, sexual intimacy can keep you off balance and keep you from healing emotionally. If this is your situation, consider telling your husband you love him and that you'd like to be intimate, but until he can make a commitment to you, it's too painful. You can tell him you need to respect yourself and protect your heart. This way you don't have to feel used or make accusations. You are simply taking a positive, proactive stand to protect yourself.

But this advice isn't only for wives. A husband may feel vulnerable as well if he has a wife who has left but occasionally craves a one-night stand with him. If you feel torn up inside from these encounters, ask the Lord for guidance about how to protect your heart.

With a heart guard in place, the time you spend together can work itself out in a kind of "friendship" and rebuild your relationship without you feeling your partner is taking advantage of you.

Safety is important for both spouses during a separation. You may feel "safer" when your partner is not wrenching your heart back and forth through a physically intimate relationship. But feeling safe is also an important prerequisite for the leaving spouse to want to return again. The safer he feels, the more often he may want to spend time with you. If you create a safe environment when the leaving partner comes over, without talking about your relationship, it can be a positive period of growth.

> 2. When a husband leaves, how do you advise a woman to be able to protect herself/family financially? If you didn't have a paying job, how did you ensure the finances be handled fairly? As a stay-at-home mom, this can be so stressful.

I know this is a big issue for many women, especially those who have been stay-at-home moms. I was fortunate that I never had a problem with this. Although I had a part-time job, my husband continued to take responsibility to support me and my daughters throughout our separation. The way I handled the finances was to send him a monthly "invoice." This wasn't something we prearranged, but I thought it preferable to nagging or talking to him about the money we needed. I just typed up a list of itemized expenses and any deposits along with the balance in our account and sent it to him. He was almost more diligent about supplying the needed funds during our separation than he was prior to that.

If a wife has been dependent on her husband's income, his willingness to meet financial needs throughout a separation shows he continues to feel responsible to support his family. A wife may be able to look at this as somewhat of a temperature gauge for how likely he might be to want to reconcile. Conversely, a husband who wants to reconcile with his estranged wife will probably earn more trust from his wife if he demonstrates a willingness to help with family expenses. For marriages where the wife works at a job with an adequate income, spouses should try to make financial arrangements agreeable to both.

If you and your children are dependent on your spouse's income and your partner is unwilling to continue giving financial support, you may need to see a family law attorney to understand your options and your rights. Each state's laws are different in this area. This is not about divorce, but about protecting you and the children.

APPLYING HEART GUARDS

If your spouse is battling an addiction, if infidelity has compromised your spouse's heart, if anger or misuse of money seems out of control, or if you are suffering from abuse, your battle has reached intensified proportions. In any of these situations, you may need to apply a heart guard and put away your fear so you can speak the truth in love (Ephesians 4:15) and be ready to take the appropriate action. Abuse will be addressed at length in the final part of this chapter.

If your spouse is creating a toxic atmosphere in the home, be cautious. If you feel tempted to give in to your partner's lifestyle or accept behaviors hurtful to you and/or your children to save your marriage, seek the Lord's wisdom. Winston Smith put it well in his book *Marriage Matters* when he said, "Love says no to sin."[1]

As you prepare to make tough decisions, start by girding up your heart with God's Word and asking for his strength so you can approach your spouse with truth in a loving way. God will give you the necessary strength at the right time. Then spend time in prayer. Before you move ahead, make sure you have:

- Established a deep and solid heart relationship with God
- Begun to make positive changes in yourself
- Continued using positive and affirming words with your spouse

- Continued treating your partner in a loving manner
- Done a little research so you know what kind of action you want your spouse to take.

If you are ready to speak to your spouse, reach out to those people in your life who are supporting you during this marital impasse. Ask them to support you with prayer as you move in a bolder direction to protect yourself and children. Then, arrange a time to have a conversation with your spouse.

As you begin talking with your spouse, affirm your love and express your concern that the problem you are addressing is driving a wedge between the two of you. Let her know it prevents you from giving the wholehearted love you want to give. Then state the problem clearly and invite your partner to make a particular change so your love can thrive.

Do not expect your spouse to give you an answer immediately. Give your mate time to think it over. But if he refuses to make a change, let him know you cannot keep living with this behavior. Although it is your partner's decision to make the change or not, you also need to be purposeful about protecting yourself, and that means making decisions of your own.

Think beforehand about how to set up an appropriate and reasonable heart guard for your particular situation if your spouse refuses to change. If your wife's temper flies out of control, your reaction will be to leave the room. If your husband is having an affair and refuses to end it, you may have to ask him to leave. If a spouse has a serious addiction and refuses to address it through counseling or a support group, a separation might be needed for a time. But again, if serious abuse is taking place, go to the end of this chapter for guidance before having that conversation or taking action.

Once you have had this conversation, as hard as it may be, the next time the troublesome behavior occurs, you must be prepared to protect your heart and home in the way you determined beforehand. Be patient through this process. Give your spouse time to weigh options. If your spouse continues with the offensive behavior, apply your heart guard, but be open and willing to give another chance.

A heart guard can become necessary for a variety of reasons, many of them very serious. Two destructive issues include infidelity and addiction.

ADDICTIONS

PJ's Stand

PJ had been married to her husband, Frank, for twelve years before she realized he had a serious problem with alcohol. Having been raised by parents who typically began the evening with cocktails before dinner, her awareness evolved gradually. While she would have a drink or two and stop, Frank emptied the bottle, seeming to have no internal alarm telling him he had enough. When PJ saw negativity and anger escalating each time he drank, she began calling him Jekyll and Hyde, but still she did not link his personality change to alcoholism. In her mind, an alcoholic was a drunk lying in the gutter.

But things changed one Saturday night when her twelve-year-old answered the doorbell to see an irate policeman standing at the door with her drunken dad. The policeman had personally escorted Frank home after pulling him and his business associate over for drinking and driving. The officer was livid. For PJ, the incident caused her to turn the corner on her tolerance for the problem. She was shocked, embarrassed, and angry. She did not want her children growing up around this behavior.

During the night, she wrestled with how to address the issue eating away at their family. She still could not put a name on it, did not know it was an addiction, but the drinking had gone on too long and had worn her down. She was afraid but determined. Now that it was involving their children, it was time to take a stand.

The next morning, PJ stood in front of the bar with Frank and told him she loved him too much to allow this to continue. They could not live this way, and he needed to stop drinking. She did not want drinking in the house anymore.

"The next time you drink," she said, "I'm taking the kids, and I'm leaving."

PJ later reflected. "I was afraid because I had no idea where I was going with three little children twelve and under, but I didn't even care anymore. I couldn't continue to live this way."

Frank's Reaction

Frank was sober when PJ spoke to him, and his response was guarded. He knew he had crossed the line the previous night, and he did not want to lose his family. He also did not know if he could live up to her conditions.

"Okay," he said, "I'll think about it."

That evening when Frank came home, he fell to his knees before God. Although PJ didn't know his drinking was an addiction, Frank did. He had tried to stop and could not. He was a Christian, but drinking had become a part of his life from an early age, and he knew he couldn't stop without help. That night Frank asked God to give him the strength to stop drinking.

When Frank came home the next afternoon, he stood looking at the pine icebox they used as a bar, and said, "All right, what's it going to be, God? If I gotta have that drink, I'll start packing my clothes, and I'll be out of this house." He stood there and waited, but the gut-wrenching struggle over taking that drink was gone. Although Frank's words may not have been the model prayer, God answered his desperate plea for healing. Frank still needed more help to fully recover and he did take part in a recovery group where he recognized and took to God the original struggles that had led to alcoholism. Since then God has used Frank's addiction for his bigger purposes. Because of their experience, Frank and PJ began an addiction recovery program called His Way, which for years has successfully helped many people find freedom from addictive lifestyles.

God gave PJ the courage to confront Frank and guard her heart and her home from addiction. If you are living with someone with an addiction, however, there is no guarantee you will have the same result. But using a heart guard to protect yourself and your children gives God a chance to do the work he wants to do in all your lives—including the addictive spouse. Using a heart guard and doing the right thing is not just about getting the result you desire. It's about honoring God with your life and allowing him to lead you into the future he has planned for you.

The Right Way to Do It

With PJ's experience, she offers solid advice for those who need to take their own stand with an addictive spouse. First, she says,

> Talk to the person in a kind way, not aggressive. It needs to be in terms of what I see objectively, not, "You're bad, you're doing this," not pointing fingers.
>
> For instance, say something like, "It seems like I see you drinking a lot. I see you drinking every night." Or "Let me tell you what I see. I see you staggering. I hear slurred words. I see you drink everything at the table till it's gone." You talk about "I see," or "I hear." You give your spouse a chance to take a look at it for themselves.

After presenting the problem to your spouse, PJ suggests you say something like the following:

> Please get back to me within a week, and we'll talk about it and see if we can problem solve or look at some options.
>
> If his or her immediate response is, "I don't have a problem, etc.," you just repeat what you said. "I hear you, but I want to meet back with you in a week and see if you've thought about it and prayed about it. We can talk about it again then and see if you think of it differently within a week."
>
> If he continues to argue, you repeat yourself and tell him, "I'm hearing what you're saying, but I still want to meet back in a week and see if you still feel the same."
>
> If he refuses to make a change when you meet the following week, then say, "Okay, well, I have to look at my options. If you're not willing to stop drinking, then drinking becomes your number one focus in your life. It no longer lines up with

God and then me so I have to decide what I'm going to do next."

It's no longer a "we" thing because he's not joining you as a team. So, you have to decide, okay, what am I going to do?

If you come to this point, PJ recommends getting legal advice—not for the purpose of divorce—but to know your rights and understand how to best take care of yourself and your children. She also recommends joining a recovery group for support. Celebrate Recovery offers tremendous support for many kinds of addictions and can be found in many churches throughout the country.

Addiction is a serious issue, and a spouse often needs to take a stand to keep it from strangling life from the marriage. Addictions have many faces: alcohol, drugs, pornography, gambling, and more. Each of these bring toxicity to a marriage, and the innocent partner needs to face the truth about what is happening with a willingness to take necessary steps to bring the matter to a resolution.

INFIDELITY

Infidelity is perhaps the most heartrending trauma a marriage can endure. Knowing how to respond to a spouse's unfaithfulness, once discovered, presents agonizing alternatives. If your spouse has committed adultery, before deciding what to do, first take your situation to the Lord. Let the Lord guide your steps as you consider the options.

Dave Carder in his book *Torn Asunder* encourages the betrayed spouse to confront the straying spouse as soon as the adultery comes to light.[2] He contends that simply bringing it to the light can begin the process of healing and restoration.

James Dobson, in his book *Love Must Be Tough* illustrates what happens when the betrayed spouse tolerates, rather than confronts, the betrayal.[3] He interviewed three women and one man who put up with unfaithfulness in their marriages for years. Despite their sacrifice and extended time of suffering, their marriages still ended in divorce. Dobson uses these stories to demonstrate that when unfaithfulness is taking place, tolerance is not only self-defeating but can actually contribute to the downfall of the marriage. Conversely, confronting the betrayal straightforwardly and courageously can set steps in motion that restore and heal the marriage.

When confronted, if the unfaithful spouse is resistant to ending the adulterous relationship, the betrayed spouse should be prepared to use what Dobson refers to as "tough love." You can couch it in terms like the following:

- You love her, you want to spend the rest of your life with her, but you respect yourself too much to share her with someone else.
- You cannot accept unfaithfulness on her part.
- She must choose.
- You are giving her the freedom to choose.
- You cannot make her do anything.
- If she chooses you, then she must cut off all contact with the other person.

When you have this conversation, be prepared to let your spouse leave if he chooses the other relationship. Spend time with the Lord beforehand so God can strengthen your heart, and try to enlist backup support from at least one Christian friend. Be patient as your spouse weighs his options. If your spouse does not choose you, then act upon the consequence you have determined. For many people in this situation, the consequence is to ask your spouse to leave.

We do not live cookie-cutter lives. One answer doesn't fit everyone. Jim Conway, author of *Men in Midlife Crisis,* for instance, recommends taking a more nuanced approach if you suspect a midlife crisis is underway.[4] What works in one situation may not work in another. God wants his children to come to him individually to seek his guidance for each particular circumstance. Keep in mind that this is also a spiritual battle. An affair can be like an addiction. Even if your spouse wants to cut off the relationship, he may be drawn back into it because of addiction to the relationship. Spiritual warfare prayer is very important. In the support team you have built around you, ask others to join with you in spiritual battle as they pray for your marriage.

If your partner decides to stay, he needs accountability, either through a pastor, a counselor, or a mature Christian friend. Reading together the book *Unfaithful* by Gary and Mona Shriver can help you understand each other and make good decisions about moving forward.[5] Also, counseling with a skilled marriage therapist (see chapter 5) or attending a marriage intensive can help you heal and reconcile the fractured relationship.

If the relationship has been sexual, you should insist your partner be tested for AIDS and STDs before you have sex together again. In this culture, it is literally a life and death matter of importance to protect yourself from sexually transmitted diseases by making this requirement. You can read more on this in the book *Back from Betrayal* by Jennifer P. Schneider, MD.[6]

ABUSE: A LEGITIMATE FEAR

In the many emails I receive, some come from women who are fearful of their husbands, and although they feel unsafe, they believe God wants them to remain in the home. Sometimes fear comes from a person's own insecurities or past histories and needs to be addressed through counseling or other programs that can help build confidence, self-esteem, and trust in God's provision. But at other times, the fears are founded on real-life physical threats or behaviors that threaten actual danger to the safety of the home for both the woman and any children present.

Other times I get emails from men whose wives have left and threatened divorce, and in their stories, I sense a feeling of remorse or regret over past abuses that took place in the marriage. Often these men say they are repentant and sorry and want their wives back, but their wives are resistant.

Too many stories of domestic violence permeate the news for this subject to be ignored. This serious but often secret and hidden agony occurs in too many homes.

Fighting for your marriage does not mean staying in situations where physical abuse is taking place. If you are afraid of your spouse or if your spouse has been abusive, look to God for guidance and find comfort in his love and provision throughout your situation. He is here for you, and he wants to make you strong. "But you, God, see the trouble of the afflicted; you consider their grief and take it in hand" (Psalm 10:14). Reconciliation is possible—even in the most severe situations—but heart guards must first be set so both spouses get the help they need.

To enlighten myself about abuse dynamics, I sat down with John Tardonia, MA, LMHC, who oversees the Pastoral Care and Counseling Center at Northland a Church Distributed, a large church in Central Florida. As a counselor who has dealt with an increasing number of abuse cases, he shared information that I believe can help those of you who find yourselves entangled in such a relationship.

Research shows that when physical abuse takes place, it often escalates in intensity and seriousness over time until and unless intervention takes place and the offender gets help.

WHAT CONSTITUTES PHYSICAL ABUSE?

According to Tardonia, any intimidating physical contact that makes a person feel trapped is considered physical abuse. This includes pushing, choking, holding the arms tightly to prevent escape, blocking an exit, or throwing things at the spouse. Of course, it goes without saying, that any kind of hitting, kicking, or assault is definitely a form of physical abuse.

The sad reality is that many spouses who are victims of physical abuse minimize the experiences and, even if taken to the ER, may resist reporting it as such because of feeling threatened. Physical abuse not only harms the individual physically, but the person's emotional sense of self is diminished as well.

Because of not feeling worthy, an individual may excuse the abuse by saying, "It only happened one time," or "I kind of instigated it. I made him mad." The abuser often makes the spouse feel as though he or she deserves the abuse.

Why Does a Person Often Stay in a Situation with an Abusive Spouse?

As an abused spouse's sense of self and worthiness continues to diminish, her ability to make the tough but necessary decisions to seek protection from the abuser becomes more difficult. Often, the abusive spouse is very skilled at making the victim feel that everything is her fault and that the abuse is justified. An abuser may make a spouse feel crazy and try to keep her isolated. You need to remember God himself is against all forms of abuse. He has many strong words to say about those who abuse others.

What Steps Should a Spouse Take if Experiencing Physical Abuse?

Fear is usually an overriding emotion, making spouses feel trapped and keeping them silent. If you have experienced physical abuse, here are some steps to take for your own protection. The safest thing to do is call an abuse hotline. A national abuse hotline in the United States is 1-800-962-2873. The counselors on the hotline can educate you, give you resources, and tell you places to go, regardless of your current location. In addition to making this call, Tardonia suggests the following steps to help disengage yourself from the abuse. These do not have to be followed in any particular order.

- Find someone safe with whom you can talk. A counselor or pastor in the church may provide a safe place where you can talk and find assistance.
- If and when abuse is actually taking place, call law enforcement immediately. Yes, this means calling the police. They will be able to assess the situation and give help.
- Find a safe place for yourself and the children.
- A restraining order needs to be obtained. This will put in place a legal restraint to keep the abuser away from you.
- Get support and connection in the faith community where you can heal and grow a sense of self and dignity and learn how to take care of yourself and the children.

IS THERE HELP FOR THE ABUSER?

If abusive spouses realize they have been abusive to their partners and want to change, what can they do to stop the abuse and hopefully save the marriage?

Often there is something in the abuser's background that has caused this individual to become abusive. Spouses who abuse may have a deep sense of insecurity. They may have been abused themselves. Being able to control those around them makes them feel more in control and gives them a sense of power.

If spouses realize they have been abusive and want to change, they need to get counseling immediately and/or join an anger management group where they can begin to work on the issues in their lives that cause them to abuse others. They also need to have accountability and make restitution, if necessary.

Can an Abuser Change? And Can an Abusive Marriage Be Restored?

An abuser can change, but it will take time. Both the victim and the abuser need to give the process all the time it needs.

If a repentant abuser wants to save his marriage, he should take the initiative to pursue counseling and be willing to share his plan with his wife.

Once victims become stronger and regain their sense of self-respect, and if they choose to forgive and work toward reconciliation, they need to make their expectations for change clear. They need to express their expectation that their spouses receive either weekly counseling or group counseling before taking serious steps toward reconciliation, and they need documentation to confirm their spouses are following through to get help. Before reconciling, it is important to make sure real change has taken place.

Victims of domestic violence also need to be discerning. Tardonia points to Hosea 7:14 as a picture of true repentance versus false repentance. When God longed to restore Israel, he lamented over the people's lack of true penitence and remorse. "They do not cry out to me with sincere hearts. Instead, they sit on their couches and wail" (NLT). Yes, in both these cases, tears can come, but in one case the sorrow comes from the heart with a desire to change. But in the other case, the tears simply come because the person regrets losing something he wants. This second person is sorry not with a heartfelt sorrow, but with a temporary lament that may even be manipulative.

The amazing truth we learn in God's Word is that he loves his children even when he finds them in the darkest places. He wants them to turn to him so he can restore them and make them whole. When they are weak, then he is strong. He will give them all they need. Second Corinthians 12:9 says, "'My grace is sufficient for you, for my power is made perfect in weakness.'"

HEART WORK

1. Read and meditate on Proverbs 4:20–27.

2. If you have decided you need to set a heart guard for protection, spend a concentrated time reading the Bible and praying each day to strengthen your heart. Ask God to help you decide on the appropriate action and how to approach your spouse.

3. If you are dealing with a serious issue that needs a heart guard, talk to a pastor, a counselor, or find a mature Christian friend to support you.

4. If you have an addictive spouse, begin attending a recovery group of some kind, such as Al-Anon or Celebrate Recovery.

5. If you are afraid of your spouse, reread the section entitled "Abuse: A Legitimate Fear." Honestly determine whether you are in an abusive situation that needs intervention. If so, take the necessary steps that lead to getting help for yourself and your spouse.

Chapter 12

Dating as Friends

My husband and I are doing better; however, still not reconciled. We have become friends again. His heart seems to be softening. — *Audrey*

I have made huge changes in my life, and my husband agrees with that. We have been seeing each other and spending time together throughout our separation, and for the most part we've enjoyed each other's company. My husband says he doesn't love me as his wife right now and doesn't know if he ever will. He says he only loves me as a friend. I've been willing to wait on God to see what he can do, but I feel I need a little something to hold onto. — *Stephanie*

She wants to be friends and is not looking to ever reconcile. Throughout our marriage I have not treated her right so I don't blame her, but when I think about it, I believe that we could have a great life together if I get myself together. I wanted to know if you have any pointers on what I can do in the meantime? — *Hal*

Being separated can take a person down so many different roads. None is easy, and few are predictable. Every new juncture requires a new decision, and every decision is fraught with uncertainty.

Every now and then, I receive emails from people who are separated, telling me that although their spouses say they are not in love with them anymore as husband or wife, they want to spend time together and be friends. Sometimes, the couple is already spending time together, and they are somewhat surprised that they are having a good time. But for the spouses who want reconciliation, this time can also be painful. They want more in the relationship. The feeling of rejection, the uncertainty of their future together, and not feeling the love of their spouse weighs heavily on their hearts.

The question becomes, *Can you just be friends with your spouse when you are separated? Are there any positive or negative consequences from choosing this path?*

When I receive these questions, my mind immediately goes back to a similar period during my husband's and my separation. During the last year of our three-year separation, my husband and I spent time together as friends. We went to movies and dinner and had lots of date-like outings. Interestingly, these "dates" were more varied and creative than times we had spent together for the past several years prior to our separation, and we actually had fun together. In one sense, it was painful because we were still separated, and I did not know what was going to happen with us in the future, but in another sense, it gave me hope and a measure of safety because I was not investing myself in the relationship physically.

We were not making commitments or promises, and we did not talk about our relationship at all—not during that whole period of time. We were not talking about our issues or what we were going to do in the future. We simply enjoyed each other's company and accepted each other as we were. That was a big step for me because my husband was still unsure of who he was and what he wanted. By this time, however, I had learned a lot about the need to simply accept him and show respect while listening to ideas that may be counter to mine and not necessarily what I wanted to hear.

For a number of years after Marv's and my reconciliation, neither of us really understood the significance of what had happened during that time of friendship. It seemed a little strange, actually. It was only after hearing a talk by Dr. Robert S. Paul, who is now vice president of the Focus on the Family Marriage Institute, that we had one of those lightbulb moments; we realized what we had created for each other was a safe place.

SAFETY

When crisis has rocked your marriage and hurled you and your spouse overboard, you may feel yourself sinking in hopelessness, but a time of safety can begin to restore trust and a new appreciation for each other. A period of friendship can provide that safe harbor when you spend time in each other's company and learn to enjoy each other without having to deal with the issues that tore you apart.

If you are the spouse-in-waiting, it is extremely painful when your partner cannot give you the answers you want to hear. You want so much to hear them say, "I love you," or "I'm so sorry. I've been a fool," or "I've missed you and I want to get back together again." But if your spouse has entered a time of honesty and openness, he simply cannot say that. As hard as it may be for you to accept this, if you can keep seeking the Lord and let the Lord's love sustain you, you may still decide to accept her offer of friendship. Then, with God's help, you can weather this barren wilderness of emotional connection so the two of you can walk in the same direction as friends and hopefully build something brand-new together.

If your spouse still seems to be in that never-never land of confusion but nevertheless wants to spend time with you as a friend, a time of friendship with you may provide a soothing balm and a bridge to healing for him. But friendship will require wisdom and strength from you. If you can be that someone who cares enough to listen to your spouse's jumbled thoughts without criticizing or judging, the two of you—together, with God as your anchor—may be able to rediscover the real person inside of him.

STRENGTH FROM THE LORD

Building a friendship with a separated spouse is not something you can do alone. You will need to spend significant time with the Lord each day to give you strength. And it will help to have a friend or two or a counselor to encourage you. You will need the Lord's undergirding love and strength to hold you up while you try to understand your spouse's fragile condition and refrain from demanding something that she is unable to produce. You will need to see with God's eyes if you want to be that silent encourager who believes in your spouse enough to pray for her and believe with her so she can make it through this time and come out on the other side as a whole person.

If your spouse desires to spend time with you as a friend, and if—while spending time in prayer—you feel this is the direction God is leading you, be prepared to do lots of listening. Let your spouse tell you his crazy ideas. Let your wife tell you what's wrong with everyone and why you two are so incompatible. Take walks together. Go out and have fun together. Talk about fun things you have done in the past and others you might do together in the future. Laugh about funny things you remember. Tell him things he did in the past that evoked your admiration. Encourage her.

Begin a friendship connection. But I encourage you to protect your heart by keeping it a friendship from A to Z and avoiding sexual intimacy. Straddling both sides of the line can keep you off balance and tear you up inside. During this time, neither of you has to live up to expectations you simply cannot meet. As you give up your expectation to hear your spouse's words of love, your spouse also cannot expect you to be physical. You have the freedom to say no. If you continue to entangle your emotions with your mate by having a physical relationship, you may be endangering your emotional health and taking away the safety required for your relationship to heal. The pain of damaged emotions may only complicate any restoration between you. If you can learn to appreciate each other on a friendship level in a safe environment, love may begin to grow again. A word of warning, however: If your partner is continuing in another relationship, friendship dating is not for you at this time.

HOW IT WORKED FOR US

For my husband and me, neither of us felt pressured. Yes, we had to live with the pain of where we were, but this only increased our awareness of our need to depend on the Lord totally for strength and for feelings of adequacy and worth. I had to remind myself on a regular basis that God was the only one whose love I could always depend on, and his love was enough. It made me continue to focus on God and grow deeper in my faith.

God used our friendship relationship to convict each of us about changes we needed to make and to reinforce in us the changes he had already begun. By spending time together, my husband could see in real time whether the changes I had made were permanent. It helped him develop the confidence he needed to move toward reconciliation. Likewise, I could see whether or not getting back together would bring on some of the same problems or whether my husband was making real and lasting changes.

My husband recalls an incident during this time of friendship dating that was particularly significant to him. We had gone to a movie in which a husband and wife experienced something similar to what had happened to us. When we came out of the movie, he dreaded my reaction, fearing I would bring it up to him. But, he says today, "You were very wise and didn't say anything. That was huge."

After learning to enjoy each other without expectations through this period of friendship, our feelings for each other began to return. Then that magic moment came when we were laughing together after a firm Christmas party. He grabbed me and kissed me. We melted into each other's arms, and from that moment on, we knew we wanted to get back together. A month later we went to a Retrouvaille weekend where we were able to express some buried and unspoken feelings in a healthy way and dive into the beginnings of a revived relationship.

A FOUNDATION OF FRIENDSHIP

If you and your spouse begin a time of friendship, this will be a time for you to be able to live out the changes God has been making in each of you without mixing it up with the expectations you have in normal everyday married life. In this time of friendship dating, you can begin to establish a friendship connection, which may have been crowded out by the pursuit of romance in your early dating days when you first met. In this fast-paced culture, romance sometimes advances quickly and squeezes out a more platonic relationship.

Recall activities you used to enjoy together and begin doing them again. Discover new interests you have in common and explore these new adventures together. Laugh and have fun without worrying about what will happen in the future. Building a firm foundation of friendship may be the beginning of something new and more fulfilling, allowing for better communication and more honesty between you.

If you look back over the stories of reconciliation in this book, most of these couples experienced a tenuous period of spending time together before they restored their marriages. But in each case, that only happened after the waiting spouse was able to completely let go. Only then could that safe time truly be safe for both spouses, without expectations. For those who successfully renew their relationships, there seems to be a natural and healthy fear, which is only overcome through a time together of safety.

But if you are the spouse in waiting, do not be the one to initiate this by suggesting you spend time as friends. If you feel God leading you in this direction, pray for God to open a door where it is appropriate to invite your spouse to do something together. For me, it was inviting my husband to help pick out the food for our daughter's wedding reception. I had no idea it would lead into a time of friendship dating, and I had no desire for it, but God knew. God led me to take that step. From there, my husband took the initiative. The pleasant time we had together felt safe enough for him to try another, and then another, and throughout the year that followed, God worked his plan for us to come together again as man and wife.

I cannot guarantee this will happen to you, and I am not suggesting you should pursue this yourself. But as you stay tuned into God's leading and allow him to keep your heart secure in the safety of his forever love, keep your eyes open. Listen to his voice and tiptoe into his grace if he begins to open doors to healing.

HEART WORK

1. Spend a day with God in prayer. Select a special place to do this and take your Bible and your journal. Use Psalm 46:10 to begin the day. Then meditate on Isaiah 40 and spend the morning and afternoon following numbers 2–7 below.

2. Read Proverbs 3:5–6. What does this Scripture mean to you right now in your situation? Ask God to open your heart to these words and listen to what he is telling you. In your journal, write a personalized message from God about what you think he wants to say to you about this Scripture.

3. Have you and your spouse been able to create safety between you when you are together? What can you do on your part to make things safe between you?

4. List three or four things you and your spouse used to enjoy doing together.

5. Spend at least thirty minutes praying for your spouse and reading Scripture while asking God to give you a deeper understanding of your spouse's needs.

6. Go back and review the notes you took about the needs of your partner in chapter 4. Add these questions to your list. What is most important to your spouse? What are his goals? What is her love language? If you don't know the answers, let this be a topic of discussion when you're together.

7. How have you let go? What are you still struggling with in regards to letting go? Review Psalm 46:10 and Isaiah 40, then write your answers to this question in your journal.

Chapter 13

Knowing If It's Time to Reconcile

We have been separated for three years now. I know you must know from your own separation how tough the road has been. Without a doubt the Lord has been changing my heart. My wife and I have been sharing together for some time now. She says she's coming home today. If I may ask, as you feel the Holy Spirit leading you, could you please pray for us? Thanks. — *Tom*

We've prayed for it, we've dreamed about it, we've longed for it, and we've fought for it. And when we hear those long-awaited words come from our mate's lips that he or she wants to reconcile, our heart leaps with joy.

After the initial euphoria, however, the prospect of actually getting back together can be a bit scary. While a separation has been painful, spouses may not be sure how to merge their separate lives together again.

In the last chapter, I told you about the friendship my husband and I enjoyed during the last year of our three-year separation. And I told you about the dramatic kiss that made us realize we wanted to get back together. But what happened after that kiss? While we knew we wanted to live together again, frankly, both of us were scared to do it. We were getting along so well while living apart, and we were both afraid of falling back into old patterns if we moved back in together.

At this point, our dating became more serious, and we started talking about our relationship. Then we attended Retrouvaille. During that weekend, each of us discovered how to express feelings we had been afraid to share with each other. In the final session, Retrouvaille leaders cautioned those of us already separated not to move back in together immediately but take time to grow in our relationship during the seven weeks of follow-up sessions. During those weeks, we used the new communication tools they taught us and gained more confidence. Those seven weeks provided more safety to jump-start some honest sharing so we could learn to trust the changes in each other, shed our fears, and live together again. Retrouvaille proved to be the catalyst that enabled us to restore our marriage.

REAL CHANGE

If you and your spouse are thinking about reconciling, spend time talking together about your relationship to make sure real change has taken place in each of you. Share honestly with each other what you have learned during your time apart. Share your hopes and dreams. If a separation took place, something in the marriage was broken. If you have matured during your separation by seeking God and allowing him to make changes, neither of you will want what you had before.

Resist the urge to reconcile prematurely. When you have endured a desperate time of loneliness and the gut-wrenching fear that your spouse will never want to reconcile, you may feel tempted to move in with your spouse immediately. But take the decision to God in prayer. If real changes have not been made, getting back together can simply revive the old problems that drove you apart previously. Do not rush reconciliation. Change takes time.

If you are the spouse who left, realize your mate may need to test the waters. Even if your spouse sees changes in you, she probably wants to make sure those changes are for real and not just a ploy. If your husband has been badly hurt, the wounds may have caused him to turn his feelings off for a time. Those emotions may need time to heal.

Keep pressing into the Lord and continue growing closer to him so you are not dependent on what happens with your spouse. Let God buoy up your heart with his peace and grace. Before victory comes, there is usually a truce and some time for negotiation.

A HEART RELATIONSHIP TO GOD

Before reconciling, consider whether both of you have established a heart relationship with God. If one of you is still wandering in a spiritual wilderness, you will be rebuilding your marriage on sand. Feelings can change again. As you look toward restoration, building your marriage on the rock of Jesus Christ can save you from opening yourself up to more potential hurt down the road.

If a spouse has left to pursue a sinful or rebellious lifestyle, it's important for that person to have a spiritual awakening before you consider reconciliation. Without an encounter with the Lord, the one who left may have little to give you. Chances are, even if he wants to reconcile right now, your reconciliation could easily fall apart again. If your partner has left and now wants to reconcile, guard your heart and wait on the Lord (Isaiah 40). Use this time to grow closer to God and be sensitive to his leading. God's love is ever-present and can hold you up during those hard times. You will not be alone. Trust the Lord to show you the way.

THE HARDEST MOUNTAIN: TRUST AND FORGIVENESS

For some of you, finding forgiveness and rebuilding trust will be the hardest mountain to climb on your road to reconciliation and healing— particularly if infidelity or addiction has been part of your story. Simone sent me an email that illustrates both the struggle and the victory of a marriage in the early stages of renewal when unfaithfulness has taken place:

> Your book brought calmness and purpose in the torment after my husband walked out on our marriage for another woman. It's also bringing me peace in the tough times as God (praise Him) restores our marriage and family. I'm trying to avoid drinking from the poisoned chalice of bitterness and instead fixing my eyes on the true cup of salvation.

People are reading your book and your blog on some of the toughest days of their lives but, through your work, God is truly saving marriages. Hopefully mine is included in that number (once I get off the fruitless cycle of comparing myself to "her" rather than giving thanks for the wonderful woman God made (me!) and let go of the overwhelming fear that my husband will betray me again. It's been six months since we've reconciled and it is getting easier day by day. I know that even if my husband can't give me what I need right now, Jesus can.

Simone

In this email, it's apparent how Simone wrestled with the pain still clinging to her heart. But she recognized the temptation to let bitterness destroy her opportunity for healing and restoration. While she had decided to forgive, Simone had to continue to fix her eyes on Jesus, and when fear raised its ugly head, she reminded herself that Jesus was enough.

Forgiveness is a process. When you forgive, you make a decision to forgive, but your heart may need time to catch up with what your mind and spirit have chosen to do. Each time those feelings of betrayal resurface, you must once again relinquish the pain to God.

In turn, the ones who have been forgiven must also be patient and willing to give grace back to their spouses when forgiveness temporarily dissolves into painful confrontation and questioning. Forgiveness takes time, and both parties should be patient with the process.

One false expectation the errant spouse may have is that once forgiven, trust will be resumed immediately. However, forgiveness does not automatically result in trust. Forgiveness is a product of grace. Trust must be earned.

If you have been forgiven, do not automatically construe that to mean your spouse will now begin to trust you again. When people have been badly hurt and betrayed, they often find it hard to trust themselves and their own judgment.

They think, *How can I trust myself to know what to believe when I couldn't see through the lies before?* You will regain trust once again through honesty, openness, transparency, humility, and accountability. When confronted, instead of being defensive, answer questions honestly and be willing to apologize once more. Be willing to share your passwords, emails, and text messages. Humble yourself before God and your spouse.

MICHAEL AND KATHERINE'S STORY

Michael and Katherine's roller coaster separation and reconciliation story provides a glimpse into some of the dynamics that sometimes take place before a couple can successfully get back together. As God worked in their individual hearts on his own timetable, they found out what it looks like to reconcile both the wrong way and the right way.

* * *

Breakfast was over, and the aroma of coffee still lingered throughout the house. Michael sat on the hearth of the fireplace in their bedroom.

"I need to talk with you for a few minutes."

Katherine perched on the edge of the bed. "What's up?"

"I'm not happy. I'm leaving. I'll be moving out soon."

"Michael, what are you talking about?" Katherine said. "Stop kidding around. That's not funny."

Michael looked up at her. "No, I'm serious, Katherine. I'm not joking. I'm leaving you."

Sitting on the edge of the bed, looking at the man she'd been married to for twenty-seven years, Katherine's world suddenly started closing in on her. What was he saying to her? *I'm serious, Katherine. I'm leaving you.* The words went round and round in her head. And with those words and the shock they brought about, the roller coaster nightmare of the next four years began.

Katherine and Michael had married young. Still in college at the time, their relationship had immediately slumped into second place as Michael's ambitious aspirations to become a neurosurgeon surged into first and became a priority in their life together. Because of the stressful demands and tight structure of his doctoral studies, they each began to live two separate lives, committed to their marriage, but not to each other and their relationship. When the children started coming, every milestone of one of their births mirrored a different milestone in Michael's academic rise toward achieving his goals. One child born in medical school, one during his residency, and another while studying for his boards.

When Michael began his profession, the frantic pace continued with long hours at work and Katherine pouring her life into the children. No time was set aside for building a husband and wife relationship. At Michael's thirtieth high school reunion, he struck up a friendship with an attractive classmate, which reinforced the discontent percolating within him. Soon afterward, Michael announced his intention to leave.

Katherine immediately reached out to Christian friends for support, knowing she was entering into the spiritual battle of her life.

"I was tested and tried and began a journey into change I never would have believed," she says. "I was learning to pray and wait on God. I knew Satan wanted to destroy our marriage, our home, our family, our reputation, and especially our testimony. I was learning about who I was—prideful in my own strength and abilities, and a people pleaser. God would rip that pride away from me and humble me to the point of minute-by-minute dependence on him alone. . . . I also learned God is bigger than I ever thought he was."

Even though Michael had no hope for the marriage, he agreed to go to counseling and began reading multiple books on relationships. He knew he did not want to be married to Katherine, but as an achiever, Michael also did not want to admit to failure. His confusion and depression kept him off balance as he groped to find a way forward.

"There was nobody else I wanted to go to or be with," Michael says today. "I just didn't want to be with her. That was my overwhelming thought for a long time." Michael decided to file for divorce, thinking it might be a way to bury the old and discover the new.

Katherine searched her heart, desperately trying to understand why Michael needed to do this. Even as he filed, he began to tell Katherine he loved her and wanted them to be together. Bewildered but anxious to restore their marriage, Katherine followed his lead. From the books she had read, Katherine suspected a midlife crisis. Seeing Michael not only as her husband, but also as a struggling brother in Christ, she listened to his confused thoughts and tried to offer encouraging words.

On a beautiful, still evening a few weeks later, Michael came over to the house and suggested a boat ride on the lake. As a cool breeze swept across the water, Michael told Katherine he wanted her as his wife again and suggested a romantic trip to the Caribbean as a second honeymoon. It was a wonderful moment and seemed to be the new beginning for which Katherine had prayed. They left the next morning and spent a heavenly few days at a picturesque resort. Thoughts of divorce were behind them.

During the next year, however, even as Michael became more involved with the children and helped around the house, and although they had long, hard conversations together and tried to reverse old patterns, Michael still appeared to be unhappy in Katherine's eyes. When she became suspicious about inconsistencies in his behavior and expressed her need for honesty, Michael flatly denied an affair but continued to hide phone calls and texts from her. He refused to make himself accountable to her or anyone else. At the end of that year, Katherine discovered multiple episodes of deception and realized he had been lying to her for quite a while.

The roller coaster broke into a downward slide once more. A voice within Katherine's heart seemed to be saying, "No more." Realizing he was not being faithful to her and had lied to her for so long, she was ready to walk away. She prayed for direction and talked with the godly women who had been praying with her throughout their separation. Her friends agreed with her assessment, and Katherine filed for divorce.

"Oh no," Michael said on the way home from their mediation. "Don't go through with it. Don't turn in the paperwork, I want to be married. Just wait."

Katherine felt the wheels of the car rumble onto the bridge crossing a wide expansive lake as she turned to look at Michael, dumbfounded once again at words that completely contradicted his actions. "Why should I? You are not acting like you want to be married. You might say that, but you're still involved with someone else. You're still changing your passwords. You're still having multiple email accounts. And

I ask you for your password, and you give it to me, and then you change it again that same night. So why? Nothing you are doing indicates you want to be married. If you can't be honest, then we can't be in a relationship. I know a marriage can't be based on lies." Katherine shook her head and turned to stare across the wind-swept waters of the lake at the rustic marina on the other side. Hearing Michael say one thing but doing another had finally eroded her trust.

Realizing Michael's words could not be trusted and he could not make a wholehearted commitment to their relationship, she went through with the divorce. After the marriage was over, Michael began grappling with where he found himself.

"I knew I was headed down the wrong road. I wasn't where God wanted me to be or doing what he wanted me to do. I needed to quit lying to myself."

A month after the divorce became final, Michael drove to their home and found Katherine in the kitchen. With a new humility, he asked forgiveness and told her he wanted to get back together. The roller coaster was climbing uphill again. This time, Katherine knew what she needed to require if they were ever to reconcile again. Trust would not come easy.

They went outside and sat on the patio beside the pool, where she told him what he needed to do before they could get back together. She asked him to meet with other men and show he truly wanted to change and become a man of integrity—the man God wanted him to be. "I need to see outward evidence. You need to be on a growth plan, have accountability with other men, and be consistent with a counselor," Katherine said.

But Michael was not able to commit to her requests. Every three weeks he came back to the house, asking her to reconcile, and every time she said the same thing.

"Well do you want to be accountable? Are you in a men's group? Are you ready to hand over all your passwords and not change them in your phone? Can I freely see them at any time? And are you willing to go to counseling?" Each time his answer was the same. He could not muster up the resolve to follow through with what she was asking.

One day as Michael was thinking about Katherine and how she fit into his life, it all came together for him. He had been looking to Katherine to make him happy and feel loved. But he began to see the problem began within himself. He did not know himself or love himself. No one could make him feel loved until he was able to accept himself. Everything he had read in the relationship books started to make sense. He realized Katherine was growing and changing as well, and he needed to accept her for who she was. Her loving him should not be the prerequisite for his ability to love her. As God started changing him from the inside, Michael realized Katherine was a gift from God to him. God knew what he needed and had a reason for putting them together. God had created Katherine and had chosen her especially for him. As this revelation came to him, Michael's motivation began to change. Instead of wanting Katherine to make him happy, he wanted to know how to make her happy.

A year had passed since the divorce, and Michael was insistent on seeing his now ex-wife. When Katherine reluctantly agreed, he was anxious but humble in his demeanor.

"I just have to know if there's any chance of us getting back together," he asked. "If you think there's any chance at all, I am willing to do whatever it takes for us to be married."

As his voice trailed off, Katherine's heart went to prayer. He sounded sincere. *Is this real? Is he ready, Lord? Is this the right time?* "Really?" she asked.

"I've been meeting with a group of men for a couple of months, and I'll go to counseling. Here's my phone. I just need to know from you if you think it could work."

Katherine could tell he really meant it. "If you are really willing to do whatever it takes—if you mean it—then we'll give it a try." They went to several counseling sessions and began dating and doing things together. They helped plan their son's wedding.

Six months after Michael made that commitment, Katherine accompanied some high school seniors from church to a Passion Conference in Atlanta.

On the last day of the conference after four days of Bible teachings, she felt the Lord speak to her heart, "You have been in a spiritual battle for your marriage for four years, and now I'm going to give you the marriage you've always wanted." Soaring about her was a new song about the God of angel armies standing by her side. Katherine felt the peace of God flow into her heart. Her brain flooded with pictures of Joseph saying, "What was meant for evil, God meant for good" (Genesis 50:20, paraphrased). A new revelation about their lives unfolded before her. *God was working that whole time when Satan was attacking your family. God was working things for good for the future, preparing, restoring, changing hearts and minds. He was changing your heart. He was changing Michael's heart. This will redeem your children's marriages and the struggles they will have for the rest of the generations to come.*

After she returned from the conference, she and Michael met with their three children, asking for forgiveness and a chance to have a growing relationship with them. It was another huge step toward healing. Katherine went to the same five women who had agreed with her on the divorce. Amazingly, they all affirmed her move toward reconciliation.

Three months later, Katherine and Michael remarried in a beautiful wedding ceremony on their back lawn overlooking the lake. The sun was shining.

It was only God who kept my heart open to the possibility of a new marriage with Michael. Some people thought I was crazy. God showed me that forgiveness, humility, unconditional love, transformation and reconciliation is His way. If I don't believe God can change people and transform the worst situation and make something new, then I don't believe the Gospel. And I do believe the Gospel. Reconciliation is why God came to earth as a human and showed us who He is and then sacrificed Himself on the cross to bring us into relationship with Him. As a Christian, I want to be like Christ, love like Him, forgive like Him, and see the possibilities in people like He does. I did have to accept that we were divorced and hold my head high and move on with life as God would lead me. I had idolized long-term marriage and used it as a measure of success and to judge others. God was ripping the pride away from my self-conscious, judgmental, perfectionistic persona.

Today Michael and Katherine make their marriage a priority, taking every opportunity to enjoy their life together. Michael sees Katherine as a special gift from God and calls her all through the day to keep in touch. In the first four years after their reconciliation, important milestones took place with the death of three of their parents and the marriage of their other two children.

"It's hard to imagine us going through all that without being together," Katherine says.

Since their reconciliation, Michael and Katherine occasionally share their story with those in crisis so struggling couples can avoid some of their own pitfalls and find hope. Whenever they talk about what happened, Michael reiterates those deep feelings about Katherine that he discovered during his years of turmoil. Sometimes with misty eyes, he reflects back to that time and tells his listeners that, indeed, he now knows that Katherine is God's gift to him. He loves her and does not know what life would be without her.

REFLECTIONS FROM MICHAEL AND KATHERINE

For those in the midst of reconciling, Michael and Katherine's insights might be helpful as you move forward. I asked them to reflect back on what happened to them and share their observations.

Questions for Katherine:

Why do you think your first reconciliation failed, and how do you think you should have done it differently?

The first time I was so desperate to get back together and preserve our family that I jumped at the opportunity when he expressed his desire to get back together. I thought, okay, let's go ahead and make this work before our friends and family even know we're totally separated. I didn't make sure he was ready. In hindsight, I could have said, "No let's take a longer break here. Let's just see how life is instead of dragging through another year or two of you still not knowing what you really want." I think one piece of advice I'd give to the left person is not to act really quickly. Be patient with the person who's left and give your partner an opportunity to really figure it out before trying to get back together.

Boundaries are often necessary when dealing with affairs, but getting a divorce seems like a more extreme measure. Why did you have to pull away from Michael so completely?

Words have to be backed up with actions. And that's really what it came to. He was still saying, "I still want to be married," but his actions were not saying that. I needed basic security in our relationship. I knew a marriage couldn't be based on lies, especially the lies of continuing unfaithfulness.

After you went through the divorce, what was your thought process that helped you stay open to reconciliation?

I stayed in the mode of prayer and remained open to what God would do in our life. It was out of my control. I realized we were going through a process, and I didn't feel I had to wait for everything to be perfect. If you have someone who is willing to get into a growth process and is showing a changed attitude, that is what you need to look for. Not a perfect person, not just someone who says the right things, but someone who's willing to go deep and examine their motives and do things that will help them change. That's where the most hope comes from. We need to be willing to grow and be open to changing.

On my part, I had to ask myself how I could be a safe place for someone to grow in my presence without pushing him away and without him feeling he was going to be shot down. All along I had hope. I believed God wanted us to be together. Unfortunately, this was the painful place we had to go to get to where God wanted us to be.

What would you say to the betrayed person about forgiveness and trust?

If you don't have any trust at all, you really shouldn't get back together. They have to have already started to earn your trust. Don't just listen to thoughts in your own little head. You have to have other godly people of the same sex around you, other friends who are watching and cautioning you and saying, "Do you think that's legitimate?" or, "That doesn't seem quite right." Others who are praying with you and can confirm whether it's a wise thing to do or not. Also, carefully choose who you listen to and talk to. They need to be people who are for marriage and reconciliation.

Forgiveness isn't a one-time thing. It has to happen over and over. You have to be willing to make that decision to forgive over and over and over again. And recognize that it's a process. Hopefully, the other person is willing to kind of let you go in and out of trusting them because trust has been destroyed and has to be earned back. They have to make you feel as comfortable as possible, going above and beyond what would be needed in a regular relationship. Once the trust has been broken, it takes a lot to get it back. It's hard to trust someone again, but ultimately our trust is in God. I think we have to put all our expectations on him and ask the Holy Spirit to guide us.

Questions for Michael:

What caused you to be so confused?

We don't know how to love each other. And it's like, it's over. What are we going to do? Guys don't want to be seen as failures. We leave, and we want a divorce, but we don't want to make the decision to get the divorce. We leave, we see somebody else who looks better, and that consumes everything. Those are two different points there. One is we don't want to make the decision to become a failure. And the other is, the lust of the eyes, to go after what we think we want, or what we think we deserve. It comes down to where we truly don't know how to love and connect with each other.

Nobody can say anything to initiate change in someone else. A person's internal motivation, down deep in his heart, needs to change. In my case, change came because God's hand touched my heart.

What advice do you have for the person who did the leaving to earn back trust?

Have humility. Humility to do whatever needs to be done to gain trust. You have to start with a little trust and build to bigger trust. And there's your friendship dating that helps you feel safe so the other person can believe what they're being told . . . because you've ruined trust.

What do you think the straying person must do to find his or her way back to the marriage and be reconciled?

Be willing to go to counseling. Be willing to be in a growth group, an accountability group with other people of the same sex. And be totally transparent with all your technology. Also, establish guardrails to help keep you out of trouble. Every married person needs to realize there's a potential for unhealthy friendships with the opposite sex. And so, I'm not going to lunch with another woman. I'm not going to travel with women. I'm not going to build deep emotional connections with people at work. I'm not going to start emailing friends my wife doesn't know about even though it seems perfectly innocent at the time. These things create a potential for danger, which leads to more of these unhappy feelings and poor choices.

What final thoughts would the two of you want to share with those who are getting back together after a separation?

Michael: I think the second time around, or the third or fourth time around, you understand that we all have imperfections. You still see them, but you've accepted the imperfections, and you accept the person for who that person is. But you have to have trust.

Katherine: Come to a place where you believe you can work through the problems, the conflict, the differences, and whatever you have to face in the future. Use all of the tools you have learned to improve connection and communication and embrace the process of growing and learning to really love each other.

* * *

If you have taken the time to seek God and have allowed him to make the changes he wants to make in you and your spouse, you will be ready to experience a new marriage together. Take a lesson from Michael and Katherine. Neither of you will want what you had before. Do not rush it. Change takes time. Let God lead the way.

HEART WORK

1. In your journal, write down the things God has taught you during this time of separation. Write a note of thanks to God for what he means to you.

2. What evidence of change do you see in each of you? In your journal, write down at least two ways you have changed. Write down at least two ways your spouse has changed.

3. If you have been sharing with Christian friends or a counselor during your separation, get together with them and ask for honest feedback.

4. If you and your mate are beginning to talk about reconciling, go to a quiet spot alone and spend a significant part of the day in prayer, asking God for direction. Take your Bible with you.

5. With your spouse, make an appointment with a Christian counselor. Tell the counselor where you've been and where you are now. Ask for recommendations on how to move forward.

6. Check to see where the nearest Retrouvaille is located and when weekends are scheduled. Pray together about whether to attend.

7. If unfaithfulness has been an issue, discuss with your partner the need for transparency and accountability.

Chapter 14

Learning to Live with the Same Spouse in a New Marriage

I know you hear so many heartbreaking stories and earlier this year I shared mine with you. Thankfully my story of heartbreak has become one of joy and restoration. Your book played a part in that. In July, I thought my marriage was ending. I had given up hope and called my attorney. The day after I called the attorney, my heart was breaking. God kept speaking to me and telling me to wait on him. I picked up your book that day and read how Jesus spent forty days praying to the Father. I put all decisions on hold and committed to the Lord that day that I would spend forty days in prayer, not file for divorce, and listen only to his voice.

Three days after I prayed that prayer, my husband sent me a message and said he was committing himself to the Lord and he wanted our marriage more than anything. I watched God transform my husband and do a work in my heart. As much as I wanted it all to be my husband's fault, I had a lot to work on myself. In the forty days I spent seeking God's will, he restored my marriage and brought my husband home.

Jim and I are not the same couple we were before the separation. We are so much better. My family is together at Christmas, I hear laughter in my home again, and I am so thankful for what God has done. — *Denese*

———

When I receive emails like the one above, my heart soars. Celebrating these victories when marriages begin to heal is one of the blessings of this ministry. Even while I am celebrating with these couples, however, I know they will face unexpected struggles as they rebuild their marriages. The fight is not finished. The road of recovery is not easy, and a spirit of commitment and perseverance is necessary to keep moving forward. For those of you in marriages coming back together, it is now time to apply the tools you have learned. The enemy will try to discourage you and sabotage your relationship. When you feel things slipping backwards, go to God. Fight on your knees once more.

If you and your spouse have humbled yourselves before God and allowed him to make changes, you can join as a team in this battle. "One standing alone can be attacked and defeated, but two can stand back-to-back and conquer; three is even better, for a triple-braided cord is not easily broken" (Ecclesiastes 4:12 TLB).

THE COMMITMENT

A few years ago, I had hip surgery. Afterward, although I immediately wanted my healing to be complete so I could return to normal life, I knew I still had work to do. My weakened muscles needed strengthening through physical therapy. After many weeks of stretches and muscle building, I began to experience long pain-free periods of normalcy. Excited about my new mobility and freedom from pain, the next time I saw my therapist, I thanked him. "It must make you feel really good to see how you help people return to a normal life."

Darren's response surprised me. "Therapists can help you," he said, "but much of the success depends on the person himself and his motivation to keep working. Some people think their surgeries should just fix it and that's that, but they don't realize they themselves need to put some work into it—sometimes *hard* work—to get stronger and functional. Some people do it, and some people don't."

His words struck me with a bigger life lesson and brought to mind the expectations of certain couples who finish our Marriage 911 class, thinking their marriages should be completely fixed or at least their spouses should be. Although some of their marriages have begun to heal, more work is still required. Recommitting to a marriage is just the beginning, and these spouses need enough commitment and perseverance to keep working so their relationship can become stronger and more functional.

If you and your spouse are recommitting to your marriage, know that hard work awaits you in the coming months. Dig down and draw up the necessary resolve and tenacity of commitment to make it over the bumps in the road ahead. Don't be surprised if you even have to make it over a mountain or two.

Commit yourselves to God and each other. If you have used the recommendations in the previous chapter about knowing when it's time to get back together, making this commitment should be a natural first step. Keep God in the center of your relationship. Spend time in prayer and in God's Word daily.

Also, take it slowly. Don't expect everything to be perfect right away. Be considerate of each other's needs, and give each other a lot of grace. Each of you have wounds that need healing. If you attended Retrouvaille, continue using the communication tools you learned there. If you have started counseling, check in with your therapist regularly.

Regardless of what else happens, do not forget to keep your eyes on the goal. Do not let things stagnate. Keep moving forward.

SAFETY

When I began writing this chapter, my husband and I sat down together over dinner to discuss it. I asked him to share his thoughts.

Safety was a big item for him.

As Marv dug into his firecracker shrimp and I enjoyed my Greek lamb and pita dish at the restaurant, we explored what it looked like to create safety in the marriage and agreed one of a couple's first objectives as they settle back in together should be making their home a safe place for each other and their children.

If you went through a time of friendship, you already began this process, but now that you are back together, safety takes a different form. You are no longer just friends. You are no longer putting the deeper issues on the back burner. You are now seeking a deeper intimacy with each other to repair the broken pieces of your hearts. How do you do this in an atmosphere of safety?

While you were separated, each of you lived your own life—separately. You made your own decisions, chose what to do and when, and set up individual routines. Now you must merge these lives together while continuing to give each other freedom to be the individuals God created you to be. Freedom as well as responsibility is necessary for love to flourish.

Each of you should give the other the freedom to be the person God created you to be, and each of you needs to take the responsibility to express your own needs. Neither of you should knowingly or unknowingly usurp the freedom of the other, and both of you should let each other know when you feel your freedom being infringed upon. Be honest. Begin creating a safety net by reading chapter 2 together and discussing the roles you have typically played in the relationship and how they may need to be modified.

Just as safety should foster honesty, honesty likewise fosters safety. Spouses feel safer when they can trust they are getting truthful information. On the other hand, if spouses expect negative reactions when they share a problematic experience or opinion about a situation, dishonest disclosures or silence on the subject might result.

Basic to everything is respect.

For each of you to feel safe in the marriage, you must feel respected. If you do not, talk about this. Let each other know what needs to change to feel respected.

As Marv and I continued discussing this over dinner, he described a situation where the wife discovered checks bouncing.

Marv suggested instead of getting upset, this wife might consider and discern if there's a more significant problem with the finances than she realized. Rather than confronting her husband with, "You told me you were going to deposit a check! Why didn't you tell me you didn't do it?" she might say in a respectful tone, "I think we need to sit down and talk about the finances. I need to understand what is happening so we don't keep having checks bounce."

Was he pulling this example out of thin air? No, in a gentlemanly way, Marv was hearkening back to a period of our life when he was a sole practitioner in his law practice. These were stressful times when business was sometimes slow and clients few. On top of this, some clients did not pay on time. Not wanting to worry me, he had carried the burden alone. But his silence kept me off balance about our money situation. When checks bounced, I became angry about his lack of candor. But his fearful anticipation of my reaction prevented him from feeling free to tell me something he knew I did not want to hear. It was a vicious circle. Neither of us felt safe.

Instead of immediately reacting to a troublesome situation, consider placing that coffee filter between your emotions and your mouth. Give yourself time to consider if there is a better way to handle the situation. Looking at the larger picture of what's happening and taking a proactive approach can not only solve the problem more effectively but also build your relationship. And if you are afraid of your spouse's reaction if you tell the truth, face your fears and take them to God. He will give you the necessary courage to build your recovering marriage on honesty and truth.

TRIGGERS

As you create a safe environment in your new marriage, sit down together and share your taboos. What triggers raise your level of irritation? You may not know what they are. If so, reflect upon circumstances that are particularly hard for you. You may want to have a counselor help you identify your triggers. If you already know your triggers, share them with your spouse. Chances are, your spouse does not know what your more sensitive wounds are. Sharing these with one another can help you avoid unnecessary conflict.

For my husband, triggers that immediately set him off are my using words *always* or *never*. When I say you *never* do anything around the house, he remembers that yesterday he took the trash out. So *never*? No. Another taboo for him is my questioning his process of getting to our destination when he's driving. While this has sometimes been a subject of contention, it has also become a source of laughter. He and I employ very different styles in our driving. I take the direct route. He takes the stress-free, leisurely one. Now that I understand his thinking, each time he drives us to one of our favorite Italian restaurants, I have learned to place that illusory coffee filter in my head and patiently watch him wind through lovely tree-lined neighborhoods without questioning his circuitous route.

Words are important. Reread chapter 4 together so you can meet each other's emotional needs and give each other the affirmation that lifts you up. Remember to use the coffee filter!

APPRECIATING YOUR DIFFERENCES

One of the problems Marv and I have typically had in our marriage is he expects me to think and act like him, and I expect him to think and act like me. He likes to tell me what I would like to order at a restaurant, but I am not into some of the spicy foods he likes. I expect him to enjoy yard work like I do, but he doesn't.

Appreciating individuality and different personalities can enhance our marriages, enlarge perspectives, and create more empathy and harmony. When we esteem each other's aptitudes and talents, we can work as a team. Taking personality tests can help with this. Also, recognizing the differences between men and women can completely change our understanding of why men and women react as they do and promote better communication.

Bill and Pam Farrel wrote a delightful book on this subject called *Men Are Like Waffles—Women Are Like Spaghetti*. In this book they explain how men often process life in boxes, focusing on one issue at a time while women often process life like a plate of spaghetti, the mind traveling seamlessly from one issue to another.[1] This can cause a variety of problems if couples do not understand what's happening.

One cold night in Florida, Marv lit a beautiful fire in the fireplace. We sat watching it and reminiscing about family moments around the fireplace. Suddenly, I saw a mosquito on the ceiling, stood up on the couch, and smacked the annoying varmint with a magazine.

We watched the fire some more and then I said, "I wonder if the Gator Santa Claus would look good beside the TV."

"Can't you just sit and watch the fire?" Marv asked. "We have this nice fire going and you're looking for mosquitoes and talking about Christmas decorations."

Since we were both familiar with the Farrels' book, I said, "Well, I have a spaghetti brain and think about a lot of things at the same time. I don't have your waffle brain. So, you enjoy being a waffle and let me be a spaghetti brain."

He laughed, and we went back to watching the fire. When couples can understand and appreciate their differences, they can enjoy life together without letting their expectations get in the way.

PERSEVERANCE THROUGH SETBACKS

During the initial stages of recovery from my hip surgery, I pressed hard into the exercises. Even though they were difficult and painful, I could see myself growing stronger. Then, all of a sudden, a spurt of intense pain rippled down my leg, and I wondered, *Will I ever feel good again?* The next week at therapy I asked Darren about it.

"You might have dips and valleys as you progress," he said. "You should expect to see a forward steady growth as you heal, but hurting might still return at various times. However, if you persevere it will eventually pass and the leg will get stronger. Don't be alarmed. Nothing's smooth. Just continue doing what you need to do. Persevere."

After surviving a crisis, relationships progress through the process of healing in a similar way. We learn new strategies, gain new tools to help us through the rough spots, and for a while, our relationship may even out and begin to move forward in a positive direction. But setbacks occur. Old habits rise up again. We may shake our heads, think nothing will ever change, and be tempted to give up. But if we go back and review the resources that first helped us move toward reconciliation, we may be able check ourselves. Perhaps we have forgotten to apply what we learned. If so, each of us can harness these lessons anew and start again by picking up where we left off before the setback.

As my therapist explained, nothing is ever smooth. When we expect it to be, we will be disappointed, and our reactions may show annoyance or irritation instead of patience. Those reactions will escalate the problem even more. Whenever frustration happens, take a deep breath, step back, say a prayer, and assess what is happening.

And remember, what we focus on expands. If we focus on the negative, everything will seem more negative, and we will get discouraged. If we focus on the positive and appreciate the good things now happening in our family, we can move forward with a more hopeful and upbeat attitude.

CONFLICT

Do not be surprised when conflict flares. Conflict is inevitable. And normal. The difference between healthy marriages versus unhealthy marriages is how we handle it. In his book *Love Must Be Tough*, Dr. James C. Dobson explains that, "in healthy relationships, a period of confrontation ends in forgiveness—in drawing together—in deeper respect and understanding—and sometimes in sexual satisfaction. But in unstable marriages a period of conflict produces greater pain and anger that persists until the next fight. When that occurs, one unresolved issue is compounded by another and another. That accumulation of resentment is an ominous circumstance."[2]

Before our separation, my husband and I handled conflict in the second manner described above. When things started getting hot during an argument, the tension often resulted in my husband leaving the house. When he came home, we both acted as if nothing had happened, ignoring the resentment building beneath the surface. After we reconciled, we had learned to handle conflict more positively. We still were not perfect in this, but as my therapist said, we saw "a forward steady growth as we healed."

Marv recommends inserting safety into these intensifying episodes by identifying in advance a safe place where both spouses can retreat if the argument heats up to where one or both needs a break. Retreating to a designated place and coming back later to reconcile differences can take the pressure off and eliminate fears of conflict leading to another separation or avoidance of the issue. Sometimes one or both needs to take a breather to clear the mind.

The Bible says to "be angry but do not sin; do not let the sun go down on your anger" (Ephesians 4:26 NRSV). You cannot always resolve differences immediately. Sometimes in the heat of the moment, you need to get a little distance to clear your head. But you can come back together before the end of the evening and commit to dealing with your issues at a future designated time. For Marv, his "safe place" is his office converted from one of our daughter's bedrooms. There, sitting beside his iPad and surrounded by his library of books and music, he can refresh his mind.

For me, our backyard is where I go to free my head of chaotic, rambling thoughts. It's where I hear from God and become renewed. When I not only need quiet but a way to release the adrenaline pumping through my veins, I may take a walk through the neighborhood. But then I come back, and we begin the process of forgiveness and reconciliation.

HEALTHY PROBLEM SOLVING

Approaching problems with humility provides the best opportunity for success. Philippians 2:3–4 applies this principle in relationships: "Do nothing out of selfish ambition or vain conceit. Rather, in humility value others above yourselves, not looking to your own interests but each of you to the interests of the others."

If both of you look at issues only from your own perspective, you will continue to butt heads. Humbly acknowledging your own short-comings when differences arise can motivate you to consider the other person's point of view and keep you from getting defensive.

When you and your spouse are experiencing a setback, with a humble heart, try to identify the persistent reactionary patterns that have caused you to react negatively to each other in the past. Then consider the approaches mentioned in chapter 3, which might help you change the destructive dynamics in your relationship so you can move forward together in a more constructive manner. Are you truly listening to each other? Do you need to validate your spouse's feelings? Is negative body language or tone of voice communicating different things to your spouse than you intend? Do you need to laugh together more? If you feel you are misunderstanding each other, perhaps the clarification technique discussed in that chapter might help. Finally, discuss how you can do a better job of acting as a team.

I MESSAGES

When disagreement arises, the phrasing of words can make a difference. Using *I* messages instead of *You* messages can shift a statement from sounding like an accusation to a simple and understandable assertion of feelings.

Consider the shift from *you* to *I* in the following examples:

"You make me so mad."

"You are . . . rude . . . controlling . . . selfish . . . ridiculous (fill in the blank)."

"You knew if you did that, I would get upset."

"I feel hurt when someone calls me a _____."

"I feel disrespected when someone _____."

"I feel confused when I hear _____."

Using the word *you* tends to sound accusatory and implies you are judging the other person's intentions, which can make that person defensive. Using the word *I* and explaining your feelings more specifically can promote honest understanding of what you feel and what you want to say. In fact, after making your I statement, you can use it to start a positive conversation by inviting your spouse to clarify what he was thinking or feeling.

"Help me understand what you mean by_____." You can elaborate further by saying something like: "I feel hurt when someone uses that kind of language, but I know that's not the kind of thing you're really trying to do. So, help me understand."

Try to refrain from using the words *mad* or *angry* and instead use more specific words, such as *frustrated* or *hurt* that express deep-down feelings you experience when you are offended.

Confronting problems with *I* messages reduces the tension when a difference of opinion occurs, and it can actually encourage understanding about the situation to help you reach a positive outcome.

ACCOUNTABILITY

Accountability after a separation is a smart way to keep you grounded while you work on strengthening your marriage. If you are reconciling with your spouse, other Christians can speak honestly into your life and let you voice concerns in a confidential setting.

In our own reconciliation process, establishing different levels of accountability became an important component. The tools Marv and I learned at Retrouvaille helped us stay accountable and honest with each other. Once a week Marv met with a Christian friend who kept him accountable and helped him grow spiritually. We could also check in with Roger, our counselor, whenever we needed.

Particularly if infidelity or addiction has affected the relationship, accountability can help trust to build, and forgiveness to remain steady.

BUILDING ON THE ROCK

Together you are now ready to seek God as a team, committed to his ways rather than your own.

In their book *Marriage on the Mend,* our friends Clint and Penny Bragg, who were divorced for eleven years before their reconciliation, talk about the importance of praying together each morning before they set out for the day. Their testimony inspired Marv and I to follow their example, but because of conflicting morning schedules, he and I struggled to be consistent. We failed with other times of the day as well—until we tried bedtime. When we began holding hands and praying together before we drifted off to sleep, we found it a beautiful way to end the day and stay connected to both God and each other.

Keeping God at the center of your relationship prevents your marriage from slipping and sliding on the sandy cliff of self-will and shortsightedness. Find a good time to pray together, and spend time in God's Word both separately and together to refresh your minds with God's perspective.

MOVING FORWARD

A couple of months after my surgery, I was heading down the aisle of my local grocery store when I suddenly realized I was walking with a normal stride, no limp, no pain, but moving with ease throughout the store. I was thrilled. There, surrounded by boxes of cereal, I silently praised God for this miracle of medicine.

My therapist affirmed my progress. "As you heal," he said, "you will hit new levels of strength. As you become aware of it, you'll suddenly realize, 'Yes, I do feel stronger.' But it doesn't end there. At this point you focus on working toward hitting the next level."

Sometimes this happens during a period of reconciliation also. You struggle as a couple with a number of slips and slides. The good days and bad days go back and forth. Then one day you realize you have not had an argument for a couple of weeks. Your husband has not criticized you for a month. Harmony has reigned in your home. A feeling of joy and celebration washes through you. You have made progress. Of course, there is always more work to do, but it's a sign you're doing the right things. If you keep it up, you and your spouse will hopefully establish the healthy, stable, and loving relationship you have been wanting.

Healing takes time. As your relationship heals, remember to continue applying the principles you have learned. Keep up the new reactions you have set in motion, the new words of affirmation you have begun speaking to your spouse, and the new priorities that guide your decisions. But keep in mind it's not all about doing. Reconciliation therapy, like physical therapy, requires a mixture of exercise and rest. Remember to keep God in the center. Rest in him. Do not continually try to fix your spouse. If your mate falls off the wagon, pray and see if the new set of reactions you have learned can spin the relationship back on course.

HEART WORK

1. Discuss with your spouse what safety in the marriage looks like for each of you. What makes you feel safe? What makes you feel unsafe?

2. Decide on a good time to pray together that works with both your schedules. Pray together at this time every day this week.

3. Reread chapter 2 together and discuss the roles you have typically played in the relationship and how they may need to be modified.

4. Reread chapter 3 together and identify any repetitious reactionary patterns that typically cause you to react negatively to each other. If you feel you misunderstand each other, try the clarification technique. Discuss how you can do a better job of acting as a team.

5. Begin daily expressing positive words that meet your spouse's emotional needs.

6. Read a good marriage book together. I highly recommend *Marriage on the Mend* by Clint and Penny Bragg as well as *The Five Love Languages* by Gary Chapman.

7. Think of mature married Christians of the same sex to whom you could be accountable to meet with them individually for a period of time to support you in your marriage. Contact them this week.

8. Find a good Bible study to attend together.

Chapter 15

Coping with the *D* Word

My husband is filing for divorce. I don't want this at all. I'm falling apart. — *Sandy*

She is a Christian but believes that it is okay to divorce and move on. I am looking for help on this journey to restoration so if you can offer any help, I would be grateful! — *Charles*

I pray my husband will change his mind and not go through with the divorce and that there is still time to turn our marriage around. The fear that grips me when I think about if he does go through with it is indescribable. Please pray for us! — *Deborah*

Lurking in the mind of many people who are separated is a dark, dreaded fear. What if, after all the waiting, their spouse still decides to file?

When I first announced to my readers that I was writing a new book on separation and asked them to let me know if there were issues they wanted me to cover, I began getting emails and messages from them. Some of them broke my heart. Women told me about standing for their marriages for four years or eight years. Men wrestled with how to keep what seemed inevitable from happening. The fear in their words was palpable.

When something as devastating and horrific as an unwanted divorce sweeps over you, it is hard to know how to deal with the pain it inflicts. You feel at the mercy of overwhelming circumstances that threaten to shred the very fabric of your life. What you have known for years will soon be gone. The fear of that *D* word looms large. What if it happens?

God has promised to give you "a garment of praise instead of a spirit of despair" (Isaiah 61:3). He promises to "comfort all who mourn, and provide for those who grieve . . . to bestow on them a crown of beauty instead of ashes, the oil of joy instead of mourning" (Isaiah 61:2–3).

With God beside you, you can walk through this valley and make it to the other side. You really can, and the sun will be shining again. You may stumble at times, cry out in anguish, and still feel the pain burning in your chest, but you will also know the God who loves you and will never leave you still walks beside you, holding you up and keeping you together. He can give you peace that is beyond your understanding (Philippians 4:5–7).

As hard as it seems, if you are in the middle of a divorce, it is time to let your old marriage die. You need to excavate the dying roots and crumbling ruins so you are free from the hold it has on you. Only when you let the old completely die can any possibility of something new be established, even if that "something new" eventually includes a reconciled marriage. As long as your mind and emotions are holding on to even a small fragment of the old marriage, you are not severing the old so you are free to move on with God into the future he has for you. Dwelling on your marriage after a divorce is like sitting in a rocking chair, hoping it will get you to the other side of town when all it will do is rock you back and forth right where you are.

If this is where you are, allow the tears to flow. It is okay. Tears will help to drain the pain so you can lift your heart to God and let him begin the healing.

As the tears begin to subside, set some goals for yourself. You still have a life ahead of you, and you are starting anew. Do not waste the future by dwelling too much on the past. If you are newly divorced, you need to let the reality of your new situation settle. What do you want to accomplish with your life? What are your spiritual gifts and how do you want to use them? Pray about some of these things and let God steer your thoughts and your life in a new direction. If you do this, you will become a more complete, content, attractive, and accomplished person.

QUESTIONS ABOUT DIVORCE

As you grope through the ruins of a marriage collapsing around you, certain questions arise—some practical, some personal. Here are a few I have received and some answers that may help you move forward. For more comprehensive support on the issue of divorce, I recommend the book *When "I Do" Becomes "I Don't"* by Laura Petherbridge.

Attorneys

Should I get my own attorney? Although I don't want the divorce, my spouse wants to save money by doing it together. He promises it will be fair.

When facing divorce, it's important to protect yourself. Don't expect your spouse to look out after your interests and take care of you at this point. Your partner is moving on in a different direction, and you need to get advice from an experienced family-law attorney about your rights. You are in new territory and need the advice of experts so you can take care of yourself (and your children). You might also want to consider seeing a mediator and divorce-certified financial planner. Some experts suggest you take a friend with you on your visit to help you remember important details.

Reconciliation after Divorce

Sadly, I am six months divorced. However, I still hold out hope for reconciliation. Am I being foolish for still praying for my husband to be reconciled first to God and then to me?

I have had many similar questions and encountered a number of women and men who continue to hope for their marriages to be restored after a divorce. It's a very legitimate question, and I have actually seen several marriages reconcile after divorce. The most important thing is that your ex-spouse is first reconciled to God.

But when people are divorced and still hoping for reconciliation, many friends will tell them they are in denial and advise them to move on with their lives. So, what should they do? I asked Cheryl Scruggs, coauthor with her husband Jeff, of the book, *I Do Again*. Cheryl and Jeff remarried after a divorce of seven years. If you are one who is still hoping to reconcile after a divorce, I highly recommend their book. These are the questions I asked her:

> *What are the chances of a marriage being reconciled after a divorce, especially when the divorce was initiated by the other person? When is hope justified, and when is it just foolish?*

Cheryl: In all honesty, I think a marriage reconciling after divorce is tough, but I think the reason for that is because couples don't think that far ahead or don't believe it could ever happen! That's where God comes in: Matthew 19:26. It takes a couple realizing that both of them need to humble themselves and look inward to where they as a couple made some mistakes. Personally, my situation looked impossible, but God showed me that Ephesians 3:20 is real and God can do immeasurably more than we could ever ask or imagine. I think there is always hope! Foolish? I suppose there are times that it could be, but I feel God can do anything.

> *If a person is divorced, but wants to see their marriage reconciled, how can they keep hope alive without harming themselves emotionally or even physically?*

Cheryl: God showed me my main job was to pray—and pray fervently and specifically. Protecting your heart is important, so finding a good biblical counselor to walk this walk with you is key. I felt emotionally worn out many times during the seven year "wait," but God and his Word is what helped me through those tough times.

> *How long should they wait?*

Cheryl: Wow. That is a tough question. If it had been up to me, in my flesh I don't know if I could have waited for seven years . . . but it was God who kept carrying me and encouraging me. I think the most important thing here is walking so intimately with God and diligently praying for his direction. That is key.

Remarriage

As a Christian, does the Bible allow me to remarry?

In his book, *Strike the Original Match*, Charles R. Swindoll did an exhaustive study on remarriage. His conclusion is there are three occasions for which the Bible allows remarriage: I defer to his comprehensive work on finding answers to this difficult question.[1]

1. "When the marriage and divorce occurred prior to salvation" (2 Corinthians 5:17; Ephesians 2)
2. "When one's mate is guilty of sexual immorality and is unwilling to repent and live faithfully with the marriage partner" (Matthew 19:9)
3. "When one of the mates is an unbeliever and willfully and permanently deserts the believing partner" (1 Corinthians 7:15)

In the first case, Swindoll points to 2 Corinthians 5:17, "Therefore if anyone is in Christ, he is a new creation; old things have passed away; behold all things have become new" (NKJV). He also quotes Ephesians 2. Swindoll notes, "When the marriage and divorce occurred prior to salvation, I believe God grants His 'new creation' the freedom to remarry."

In the second case, Swindoll refers to Matthew 19:9, which says, "Whoever divorces his wife, except for immorality, and marries another woman commits adultery." Swindoll interprets this as a spouse who has chosen an immoral "life style," "an obvious determination to practice a promiscuous relationship outside the bonds of marriage." He does not construe it to mean a "one-time-only-experience" of unfaithfulness.[2]

Through grace, Jesus gave victimized, offended spouses the option of divorcing, but that is not necessarily the only or best decision. Many marriages are able to surmount this enormous challenge and rebuild their marriages. However, when repeated attempts have been made to keep the marriage together and the errant spouse continues in sustained sexual infidelity, the Lord grants freedom from the painful bonds that hold them together.

The third case is based on 1 Corinthians 7:12–15:

> If any brother has a wife who is not a believer and she is will-ing to live with him, he must not divorce her. And if a woman has a husband who is not a believer and he is willing to live with her, she must not divorce him. For the unbelieving hus-band has been sanctified through his wife, and the unbeliev-ing wife has been sanctified through her believing husband. Otherwise your children would be unclean, but as it is, they are holy. But if the unbeliever leaves, let it be so. The brother or the sister is not bound in such circumstances; God has called us to live in peace.

Swindoll's interpretation is that "being free of that 'bondage' obvi-ously means being free of the responsibility of that marriage. The deser-tion of the unsaved partner breaks the bond, thus freeing the believer to divorce and remarry. . . . It implies a determined and willful decision that results in leaving the relationship with no desire to return, no inter-est in cultivating that home, no plan to bear the responsibilities, and no commitment to the vows once taken. That's 'leaving.'"[3] This is not refer-ring to a situation where a spouse only leaves for a short time and then desires to return. You can find a more extensive explanation in Charles R. Swindoll's book, *Strike the Original Match*.

Dating

There is someone else in my life now, but we both agreed we can only be friends. I'm not dating. However, I have opened the door for the possibility of another relationship, even though I'm trying to be led by God. What do you think?

If you have biblical grounds for divorce, there is nothing wrong with seeing someone else after you are divorced. I'm pleased you have decided to keep things on a friendship level though. That is a smart decision. Relationships should progress slowly and start on a friendship level. But I also want to throw in a serious word of caution. If you are considering a dating relationship after divorce, be careful you are not transferring a fixation from one person to another. If you now feel good about things simply because another person of the opposite sex appreciates you, that could mean you are still not "free." This will not happen if you make Jesus your lover. He should be the one to keep your heart safe. Jesus loves you more than any dating partner will, and he will show you how beautiful, special, and valuable you are. God will show you the direction he wants you to take and help you keep your heart open to all his possibilities—even a possible reconciliation with your spouse. Keep your concentration on Jesus.

While following God should be your first consideration, the second is your children. And I can tell you, children are almost always hurt by a divorce. I have never seen it not happen. And for this reason too, I caution those who are newly divorced to wait before getting involved in another relationship.

Regardless of what happens in the future, for now it may be best to allow time and God to heal your heart. It is never good to move quickly from one relationship to another because you will merely be dragging baggage along with you into the new relationship. After a divorce, counselors and divorce recovery experts always recommend waiting a period of time before getting involved with someone new; the time is proportional to the length of the marriage.

In *When "I Do" Becomes "I Don't"* by Petherbridge, the author recommends waiting "a minimum of two years . . . to mourn the death of a marriage before dating. People who remarry within two years of their divorce have a much higher rate of a second divorce. Second, and just as essential, the children aren't ready for a stepparent. Just as you need time to mourn, so do they. Your focus needs to be on helping your kids cope with the loss they've sustained. Adding a new marriage to the gamut of emotions will only prolong their healing."[4]

I am recently divorced and just do not know how to cope with the loss. I never expected this to happen. My life is turned upside down. How do I move on?

Many churches have a divorce recovery program that can provide enormous help to you as you adjust to this new situation in life and try to find healing. I highly recommend you find one of these programs. You need support from people who can offer honest and caring guidance and understand what you are going through. Visit the Divorce Care website here: https://www.divorcecare.org/.

LETTING GO AGAIN

You've prayed. You've sought advice. You've talked and texted your friends. You've waited. All the while, you've hoped this would not happen. Yet, here it is. It's like your worst nightmare come true. But if a divorce has actually taken place, the reality of it can't be denied. You can no longer shove it into the shadows. You are forced to let go.

God loves you. He really does. In Isaiah 54:5, he has promised to be your spouse:

> For your Maker is your husband—
> the Lord Almighty is his name—
> the Holy One of Israel is your Redeemer;
> he is called the God of all the earth.

Do not fear. Wherever this road leads, God has provided. You can count on him. First John 4:18 says, "Perfect love drives out fear." When you grasp hold of God's perfect love to carry you through, he will hold you close and make you strong.

God allows people to walk through difficult times in their lives for a variety of reasons. Sometimes it's because of bad choices they have made. Sometimes it's because he wants to release them from a bad situation and help them change direction. Sometimes he wants to get their attention to show them something they have been missing. Other times it's just because he wants them to run into his arms and stay there to discover a deeper love than they can comprehend. If you need to find a new kind of hope for a different kind of future than what you have been praying for, read on. This is not the end. It is just a new kind of beginning.

HEART WORK

1. Reread chapter 8 to help you let go once again.

2. List three things you would like to do in the next few months. What steps will you take to achieve these goals?

3. Pray and ask God to help you look into the future and set a long-term goal for yourself. What might this look like?

4. If you have never taken a spiritual gifts test, ask your pastor to make one available to you, and take it now. After you take the test, write down your spiritual gifts and ask God how you might effectively use them for his purposes in the future.

5. Talk to your children and take steps to help them through this difficult time of loss. Plan something special with them—perhaps a trip or something they can get excited about. Let them help you plan it.

Chapter 16

Who Are You Holding For?

After a year of separation, my husband decided he wants a divorce. I'm taking the next month to pray and fast to see how to react and what to do. I'm trying to discern God's plan in this. — *Elaine*

Linda, many thanks for praying for my marriage. I'm sorry to say that things have gone from bad to worse. After holding on for ten months of separation my wife last week served divorce papers on me. When I received the papers, it shook my life. For some reason it completely changed me and I am now completely surrendered to the lordship of Jesus. I still believe that God can save it, but it looks very unlikely. I am fighting for her, praying so much, and have an incredible peace and hope for my future no matter how things turn out. — *Kenneth*

MY STORY

One day in the middle of our separation, I stood alone in a schoolyard where I had volunteered. With nothing to distract me, my mind wandered as usual down all the familiar rabbit holes that haunted me on a daily basis. *Why is this happening? What will happen between my husband and me? What is he feeling? Where are we heading?* Suddenly, while staring across the empty field, a new impression dropped unexpectedly into my thoughts, *Your life is not about your husband.*

My gaze lifted above the empty shadows of my fears to take in the gracefully spreading branches of the oaks across the road. The words again streamed forcefully into my mind like a light pushing out the darkness. *Your life is not about your husband.* I blinked as the thought pressed further into my consciousness.

Your life is not about your husband.

My mind came alive and the words popped. I stood entranced. It was true. My life was not about my husband. My life was more than that. I knew God was speaking to me. The words wrestled again to take a firmer hold. *Your life is not about your husband. Your life is about . . .*

"Me and God," I whispered. Darkness and shadows slipped away as a new freedom enveloped me. Yes, the sun was actually shining. My eyes opened to brilliant blue skies above, softened by white puffs of clouds drifting in the sunlight. My life is not about my husband. My life is about me and God. That afternoon was when I began to let go.

What I discovered during those turbulent three years of my separation was that it's only in the letting go that God brings about the transformation he wants to make in our lives. And what he wants to do is so much better and more fulfilling than what we thought we wanted.

If you are separated and fighting for your marriage, the death spiral of realizing God may not plan life to go your way is painful. However, in your waiting, God has hopefully brought you something more precious than what you thought you had lost—the sweet intimacy of a deeper relationship with Christ—a love that will last forever and fulfill you in ways you never thought possible. Jesus is the true lover of your soul.

Although your heart has been on hold for your spouse, it is only when you truly fill yourself up with Jesus that your heart will completely heal. He is the only one who can give you a perfect love. Whether your marriage is reconciled or not, God has a perfect plan for you. But you have to trust him. Open your eyes, and you will see that Jesus is enough.

I want to close with two stories of people who did discover Jesus was enough for them. Each story is unique as your own will be as well.

Let God finish writing your story the way he wants it to be. Trust him as those in the following two stories did.

MIYA'S STORY

Each year when we start a new Marriage 911 class, I set out a gold-plated tablet on the registration table. It reads, *They that wait upon the Lord shall renew their strength; they shall mount up with wings as eagles. Isaiah 40:31.* It was given to me by Miya, a woman in one of our first classes a number of years ago.

Miya is a beautiful young woman whose husband's heart had hardened against her after years of them hurting each other through bad choices, selfishness, and an inability to communicate their hurts. She had asked forgiveness, but he could not reach the place where he could trust and love her again. He did not divorce her. He did not leave. They simply lived in the same house as distant acquaintances.

Emotionally and spiritually exhausted, Miya came to our class to give her marriage one final chance.

On the first night, she told those in her small group, "This is my last try. If my husband won't reconcile after this, I'm filing for divorce."

Even before the class was over, however, hurtful words from her husband sent her reeling again. When she packed her bags and prepared to leave, God touched her husband's heart to encourage Miya to stay. That night as they talked, she realized her husband was a good man who had been serving at church to deal with struggles of his own. She saw God at work in both of them. The hope this new perspective gave her propelled Miya solidly into the arms of Jesus. She and her husband decided to give it another try.

Still, however, the communication barrier was not lifted. Although continuing to live in the same house, they became alienated once again and each went their separate ways.

But the open-heart surgery God had done in Miya's heart caused her to surrender her life to God completely. For the next seven years, Miya lived out the words on the tablet she gave me in her own life. She waited on God. No longer did she focus on saving her marriage. She had found another lover—Jesus. She would hold for him.

For a couple of years, she helped with registration for our Marriage 911 class, continuing to offer hope to those with crumbling marriages even though her own remained on hold. She pursued the Lord with all her heart and stayed busy both in her work and in her pursuit of God, allowing God to fine-tune her spiritual ears so she could recognize his voice when he spoke to her.

She felt led to a small church that had an emphasis on worship. Everyone there knew each other and prayed for each other. When something negative happened and she felt rejected, Miya was quick to ask for prayer. During times of worship, the intimacy of the Holy Spirit was so precious she often cried through the praise services, feeling God's love as she never had. Worship purified her so she could focus on God alone.

Miya started looking for God's blessings on her life as though she were in a scavenger hunt, proactively looking for any blessings God had given—knowing they were there and considering it her job to find them. "You don't have to look far," Miya said. "Everything is a blessing. Breathing in the morning is a blessing. Walking without pain is a blessing."

An important new leg of Miya's journey began when she traveled to Israel with her church and began to relate to the Orthodox Jews she met. She was hurting, and she knew they had a long history of hurting that was far more acute than her own. She wanted to know more about these people and understand their suffering, their faith, and how they had overcome the struggles of their past. Seeing the promises God made to Israel and how he kept them by bringing the Jewish people to their homeland in 1948 encouraged Miya in her faith to believe in God's promises for herself.

When she crossed paths with her husband at home, she occasionally shared a brief impression of what she was learning about the Jewish people. Surprisingly, he was interested, and for the first time in a long time they began to dialogue. On this subject alone, they began to connect. Gradually, their conversations expanded into a period of friendship. After a few years, he started attending her new church with her. Then they went to Israel together.

Today, two years after their reconciliation began, Miya and her husband do almost everything together. He wants her around all the time, and together they are serving God.

"Every morning," she says, "we both get up and are beside ourselves that this healing has taken place. It's like a brand-new love—way greater than it was before." They are able to talk about what they went through and almost laugh about it. "Forgiveness is paramount," she says. "You have to truly forgive. God redeemed us. There's no doubt that it's a God thing."

God has his own plan and his own timing. Not every story will end as Miya's did. Not every period of waiting, regardless of the sincerity of someone's faith, will end with reconciliation. If you are separated, God's ultimate desire and goal for you is that you embrace his heart, submit to his will, and walk with him as his child in love, peace, and joy.

If you have experienced the agony of trying to do things your own way without seeing the results you want, remember it is in the letting go that God brings about the transformation he wants to make. But you have to have faith that his transformation is the best transformation, and it may not look the way you want it to look. Life is not about your spouse. Life is about you and God and what he wants to do in your life.

No two stories are alike, but all God's stories are good stories. He is "the author and finisher of *our* faith" (Hebrews 12:2 NKJV). Like Miya, Theresa sought God with all her heart in the middle of a heartrending separation. She found what she longed for, but it surprised her by coming about in an unexpected form. Read Theresa's letter below and grab hold of Jesus's hand with a heart full of faith so he can lead you down the path he has chosen for you.

THERESA'S STORY

Hi Linda, Can you believe it has been almost seven years for me since I read your book and joined your 911 class? And yes! *Broken Heart on Hold* was literally my "paramedic" at the time.

As I read the title of your new book, I could not help but go back in time and think of how I felt at the time of my mess.

Finding you and your book on the internet gave me so much hope and literally saved me from going insane! I had been crying in the desert for quite a while, and finally my prayer was being answered! I found you, and your beautiful story of marriage restoration!

Yes! (I said to myself) If I do X, Y, and Z, God *will* restore my marriage! The phrase "on hold" from the title of your book made me think, it was a matter of not "if" but more of "when." I thought, "I'm just on hold. God will do this for me. I just have to have faith and wait on God to do His thing." I read your testimony through *Broken Heart on Hold* and every time I got out of our Marriage 911 class I thought to myself, "Aha! It happened for her and for all of the other guest speakers I've heard in class; it will happen to me as well! After all, I'm asking *God* and I know He *can* and *will* do it because He is for marriages. Right? His Word says so. All I need to do is keep the hope alive for marriage restoration until God makes it happen; that will do the trick." That was my thought process for almost four long years . . .

But after almost three years of intense prayer, I felt something inside me was changing. I was losing the battle and I knew it. I just couldn't figure out why? Was I losing hope in marriage restoration? Yes, of course. But as I was losing "that kind" of hope, I was gaining another one. God was building me up little by little. In fact, it felt like God was actually *restoring me*, instead of my marriage. So, my hope transformed. I no longer felt I was "on hold" but really moving in another direction.

So, my thinking started to shift. Like a lens trying to adjust to different images, I had to do the same. So, my questions became more self-focused. I asked, what was my battle after all? What was it I was *really* fighting for, or holding on to?

As time passed and my husband was not coming back home and moving even further from the idea of restoring our marriage, I could not help but think, "What if God is doing something different here?" For the first time I had to think about another possibility.

So, I ask you, Linda: What if I was not really fighting for my marriage? What if God was actually having me fight for myself—my soul, my heart, my own salvation? What if this is about coming out of this mess of separation and divorce, still victorious? What if God is actually preparing me for a new beginning—yes—but in another direction?

What I have learned is that with God, it's about what He wants for me, and my job is to discover His will for me. That means I need to examine all the possible outcomes, including (apparently) losing the battle. Now, does that mean I should not fight for my marriage restoration at all? Of course not! But the challenge is: How can I keep the hope, and yes, still fight for my marriage, while understanding that there is a chance God might want to do something different in my life rather than restore my marriage?

When I first encountered *Broken Heart on Hold*, my mind was so set on "saving" my marriage that I never considered the possibility that God might want to do something different in my life. But that is exactly what He did! It's been seven years since my husband left our home and four since we divorced. Seven years of the passion, death, and resurrection of Theresa! And I'm in no way trying to compare myself to Jesus's experience. But this analogy helps me see exactly God's plan for my life. I literally went through those stages together with my sweet Jesus. Of course, not the same way He did, but I assure you, I did go through those three stages. Still, no marriage restored. Why? The one that has been restored, I assure you, has been ME! I can finally hear Jesus saying to my heart, "See, I am doing a new thing! Now it springs up; do you not perceive it? I am making a way in the wilderness and streams in the wasteland" (Isaiah 43:19).

I have stayed single for the last seven years, with only one encounter with a man that ended up going nowhere. And I asked myself, "How is this possible? How is it that I have been able to stay single for such a long period of time?" I can tell you now, Linda. It is just *GOD*! He obviously had a plan in mind. Because I stayed faithful, and repented when deviating, and came back to Him each time, He has been able to accomplish much of that plan in my life. Of course, much more to come, but I have no doubt in my mind that my change in direction was God's plan.

I see so many women losing hope in marriage restoration and going about working on their own "restoration" by finding another man. Very few really understand that God won't even look at restoring their marriages nor getting them another significant other UNTIL He first restores each one of them individually!

So I'm hoping those who read *Fighting for Your Marriage While Separated* won't simply be looking for a quick fix, but understand they may encounter a deeper "prescription" to help them become who God meant for them to be. God did it for me, Linda, and He used you as the starting point. He sure wanted me to pay attention. Although, it cost me many nights of turmoil and heartache to accept there could be another possibility, God's faithfulness kept me walking through the narrow path. It's not easy, but it is the best and only right path. So let go and let God.

Love you much, Theresa

YOUR STORY

If your heart squeezes into tight knots when you see the months and years slipping by with still no resolution to your marriage dilemma—if your prayers hang in limbo—perhaps, like Theresa, yours is a different kind of resurrection story than you expected. Perhaps it is your resurrection God is after.

You began this journey with a broken heart. As we have talked about fighting for your marriage, I pray your heart has been renewed, and you yourself have experienced a transformation. For even when you began searching for answers on this winding road, Someone was waiting for you. He still is. His arms are always open.

No matter what has happened on this journey or what will happen, I pray your life will be richer and fuller as you have taken the hand of Jesus. He is not just here for this journey, but for all those journeys ahead as well. Jesus your Savior is the lover of your soul for a lifetime and beyond. "Those who go out weeping, carrying seed to sow, will return with songs of joy, carrying sheaves with them" (Psalm 126:6).

Those who hope in the LORD
will renew their strength.
They will soar on wings like eagles;
they will run and not grow weary,
they will walk and not be faint. (Isaiah 40:31)

For end-of-the-story updates and more help and encouragement, visit http://lindarooks.com or http://brokenheartonhold.com.

Recommended Resources

Abuse
US National Abuse Hotline: 800-962-2873

Addiction Support Groups
Alcoholics Anonymous: *https://www.aa.org/*

Al-Anon Support Group: *https://al-anon.org/*

Celebrate Recovery: celebraterecovery.com

Boundary and Control Issues
Dr. Henry Cloud and Dr. John Townsend, *Boundaries in Marriage: Understanding the Choices that Make or Break Loving Relationships* (Grand Rapids, MI: Zondervan Publishing House, 1999).

Dr. James C. Dobson, *Love Must Be Tough: New Hope for Marriages in Crisis* (Waco, TX: Word Books, 1983).

Les Carter, *Imperative People: Those Who Must Be in Control* (Nashville, TN: Thomas Nelson, 1991).

Counseling
William J. Doherty, "How Therapists Harm Marriages and What We Can Do about It," *Journal of Couple and Relationship Therapy* (2002): 1–17, https://dohertyrelationshipinstitute.com/wp-content/uploads/sites/8/2015/04/howtherapists.pdf.

Differences
Gary Chapman, *The Five Love Languages: How to Express Heartfelt Commitment to Your Mate* (Chicago, IL: Northfield Publishing, 2004).

Bill Farrel and Pam Farrel, *Men Are Like Waffles—Women Are Like Spaghetti: Understanding and Delighting in Your Differences* (Eugene, OR: Harvest House Publishers, 2001).

Linda Gilden and Linda Goldfarb, *Linked Quick Guide to Personalities: Maximizing Life Connections One Link at a Time* (Friendswood, TX: Bold Vision Books, 2018).

John Gray, PhD, *Men Are from Mars, Women Are from Venus: Practical Guide for Improving Communication and Getting What You Want in Your Relationships* (New York, NY: Harper Collins, 1993).

Marita Littauer and Florence Littauer, *Wired That Way Personality Profile: An Easy-to-Use Questionnaire for Helping People Discover Their God-Given Personality Type* (Ada, MI: Baker Publishing Group, 2006).

Divorce

Divorce Care support groups: https://www.divorcecare.org/

Laura Petherbridge, *When "I Do" Becomes "I Don't": Practical Steps for Healing During Separation and Divorce* (Colorado Springs, CO: David C. Cook, 2008).

Forgiveness

Linda W. Rooks, "Understanding Forgiveness," *Focus on the Family*, 2011, https://www.focusonthefamily.com/marriage/divorce-and-infidelity/forgiveness-and-restoration/understanding-forgiveness.

Infidelity

Dave Carder, *Torn Asunder: Recovering from an Extramarital Affair* (Chicago, IL: Moody Publishers, 2008).

Gary Shriver and Mona Shriver, *Unfaithful: Hope and Healing After Infidelity* (Colorado Springs, CO: David C. Cook, 2005).

Marriage Intensives

Focus on the Family's Hope Restored Program: http://hoperestored.com/

Hope and Healing for Adultery Recovery: http://www.hopeandhealing.us/

Midlife Crisis

Jim Conway, *Men in Midlife Crisis* (Colorado Springs, CO: Cook Communications, 1978).

Patrick Morley, *Second Half for the Man in the Mirror* (Grand Rapids, MI: Zondervan, 1999).

Online Help
The Couple Checkup: http://www.couplecheckup.com/

Heart Talk Blog and "End of the Story" Updates: http://www.lindarooks.com/

Marriage Help and Resources: http://www.brokenheartonhold.com/

Willard Harley's Help for Marriages: http://www.marriagebuilders.com/

Programs and Marriage Workshops for Marriage Restoration
Marriage 911: http://marriage911godsway.com/

Retrouvaille: https://retrouvaille.org/

Rebuilding a Marriage After Crisis
Clint Bragg and Penny Bragg, *Marriage on the Mend: Healing Your Relationship After Crisis, Separation, or Divorce* (Grand Rapids, MI: Kregel Publications, 2015),134–135.

Separation and Marital Crisis
Michele Weiner-Davis, *The Divorce Remedy: The Proven 7-Step Program for Saving Your Marriage* (New York, NY: Simon & Schuster Paperbacks, 2001).

Dr. Robert S. Paul and Dr. Greg Smalley, *The DNA of Relationships for Couples* (Carol Stream, IL: Tyndale House, 2006).

Linda W. Rooks, *Broken Heart on Hold: Surviving Separation* (Colorado Springs, CO: David C. Cook, 2006).

Cheryl Scruggs and Jeff Scruggs, *I Do Again: How We Found a Second Chance at Our Marriage and You Can Too* (Colorado Springs, CO: Waterbrook Press, 2008).

Joe Williams and Michelle Williams, *Yes, Your Marriage Can be Saved: 12 Truths for Rescuing Your Relationship* (Carol Stream, IL: Tyndale House, 2007).

Spiritual Growth
Catherine Marshall, *Beyond Ourselves* (New York, NY: McGraw-Hill Book Company, 1961).

Spiritual Warfare
Neil T. Anderson, *The Bondage Breaker®: The Next Step* (Eugene, OR: Harvest House Publishers, 1995).

Endnotes

Chapter 1

1. Joe Beam, "The Love Path" Seminar, Smart Marriage Conference, Orlando, 2010.

2. Glenn Collins, "Chemical Connections: Pathways of Love," *New York Times*, February 14, 1983.

3. Collins, February 14, 1983.

4. Michele Weiner-Davis, Smart Marriage Conference, Orlando 2010.

Chapter 2

1. Dr. Henry Cloud and Dr. John Townsend, *Boundaries in Marriage: Understanding the Choices that Make or Break Loving Relationships* (Grand Rapids, MI: Zondervan Publishing House, 1999) 26.

Chapter 3

1. Joe Williams and Michelle Williams, *Yes, Your Marriage Can be Saved: 12 Truths for Rescuing Your Relationship* (Carol Stream, IL: Tyndale House, 2007).

Chapter 4

1. Nancy C. Anderson, *Avoiding the Greener Grass Syndrome* (Grand Rapids, MI: Kregel Publications, 2004), 56.

2. Gregory L. Jantz, PhD, "Brain Differences Between Genders," *Psychology Today*, February 27, 2014, https://www.psychologytoday.com/us/blog/hope-relationships/201402/brain-differences-between-genders.

3. Gary Chapman, *The Five Love Languages*, (Chicago, IL: Northfield Publishing, 2004), 59.